Betty Crocker's
LOW-FAT COOKING

PRENTICE HALL

New York   London   Toronto   Sydney   Tokyo   Singapore

PRENTICE HALL GENERAL REFERENCE
15 Columbus Circle
New York, New York 10023

Library of Congress Cataloging-in-Publication Data

Crocker, Betty.
  [Low-fat cooking]
  Betty Crocker's low-fat cooking.
    p.   cm.
  Includes index.
  ISBN 0-671-88771-8
    1. Cookery. 2. Low-fat diet—Recipes.
  I. Title. II. Title: Low-fat   cooking.
  TX714.C766   1994
  641.5'638—dc20   93-38096
                                          CIP

Designed by Levavi & Levavi, Inc.

Manufactured in the United States of America

   10 9 8 7 6 5 4 3 2 1

First Edition

Contents

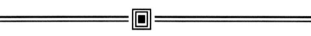

Introduction

Today, we are all interested in reducing the fat in our diet, without giving up great taste. And that's exactly what you'll find in *Betty Crocker's Low-Fat Cooking,* less fat and all the great taste you expect from Betty Crocker. All the recipes here have 30 percent—or less—of their calories from fat.

Need a low-fat appetizer? Then you'll love Black Bean Dip, Herbed Yogurt Cheese and Spicy Tortilla Chips. And when you are ready for the main course, you'll be delighted with the range of choices here.

First, there's fish and shellfish, with enticing recipes such as Halibut Stir-Fry, Apple-stuffed Sole and Seafood Pasta with Vegetables. Or choose a chicken dish such as Scandinavian Chicken with Apricots or Chicken-Basil Noodles. And if you are in the mood for a meatless dish, try Mexican Strata or Triple-Cheese Ravioli.

Looking for a meaty main dish? You'll enjoy Gingered Flank Steak, Beef Stroganoff, Caribbean Pork Tenderloin and other delicious dishes. And we haven't left out dessert! Low-fat finales such as Bread Pudding with Brown Sugar Meringue, Sacher Cake Roll, and Chocolate-Orange Angel Food Cake put the excitement back in dessert.

We have also included useful information to help you follow a low-fat diet, with ideas for low-fat snacks, shopping tips, methods for low-fat cooking and other creative ways to reduce fat in your diet. We think you'll find this is the perfect book for beginning a low-fat eating plan, as well as just what you are looking for to give you great ideas to continue reducing your fat intake. And best of all, while you're reducing fat, you won't be reducing great taste!

THE BETTY CROCKER EDITORS

All About Fat

With everything you've read or heard about fat, you may believe it's a good idea to try to eliminate it from your diet. But the truth is we actually need some fat. It is our only source of linoleic acid, a fatty acid essential for proper growth, healthy skin and the proper metabolism of cholesterol.

Also essential is the role fat plays in the transport, absorption and storage of fat-soluble vitamins (A, D, E, K). In addition, fat helps the body use carbohydrate and protein more efficiently. And finally, fat deposits—where much of the body's excess fat is stored—play an important role in insulating and cushioning the body and organs.

On the average, Americans eat about 38 percent of their daily calories in the form of fat. Health and nutrition experts recommend that people over the age of twenty reduce fat to an average of 30 percent—less than one-third—of daily calories. In a typical 1800-calorie diet, it means a drop from 75 grams to 60 grams of fat per day. You'll appreciate the recipes here, all of which have 30 percent—or less—of their calories from fat.

REDUCING FAT IN YOUR DIET

Physicians, nutritionists and researchers have developed some guides to help you reduce the amount of fat you eat.

- Eat fewer high-fat foods. Eating less *visible* fat like lard, shortening or oil is important, but *hidden* fat is abundant too. Limiting fat intake may mean eating less ice cream, fewer chips and less of creamy or cheese mixed dishes. We need to be aware of the fat in food—its type and quantity—to make choices that will keep total fat intake and calories down.

- Eat smaller portions. Remember, just because a food is high in fat doesn't mean we can't eat

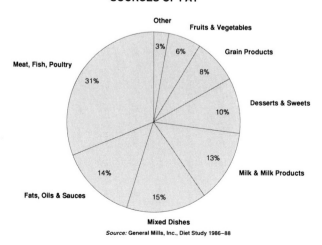

SOURCES OF FAT

Other 3%
Fruits & Vegetables 6%
Grain Products 8%
Desserts & Sweets 10%
Milk & Milk Products 13%
Mixed Dishes 15%
Fats, Oils & Sauces 14%
Meat, Fish, Poultry 31%

Source: General Mills, Inc., Diet Study 1986–88

it at all. It just means we should eat smaller servings, less often.

• Choose cooking methods that use less fat. Broil, bake, roast, grill, poach, steam, stew and microwave foods whenever possible. You can stir-fry, too, if you use small amounts of unsaturated oils.

• Use nonstick cookware. A nonstick skillet and one or two nonstick saucepans with a nonstick-cooking spray can easily lessen the amounts of fat used in cooking.

• Serve chicken, turkey or fish often. Light-meat chicken and turkey are naturally low in fat, especially if you remove the skin. Most fish is also very lean. Even such higher-fat fish as salmon are as lean or leaner than poultry and lean beef. Some fish also have the added benefit of omega-3 fatty acids.

• Choose lean cuts of meat and trim fat. There are many leaner cuts of beef, pork and lamb now widely available. Trim visible fat before cooking. (It's probably not a good idea to completely eliminate meats from the diet because they are important sources of many other nutrients, among them iron and vitamin B_{12}, that may be hard to get from other foods.)

• Use lowfat or skim milk products. Many milk products contain a great deal of fat, especially if they are made with whole milk or cream. Choose from the many lowfat and nonfat dairy products that are available. Look for skim milk, lowfat or skim milk cheeses and lowfat or nonfat yogurt. Don't eliminate dairy products entirely, because they provide the calcium needed for healthy bones.

• Limit added fats and oils to five to eight teaspoons per day. We're talking about how much butter you add to bread and the amount of dressing or mayonnaise you load on salads. Try reduced-fat margarine and dressings. Remember, there's no need to give up fats completely. but we do need to be aware of how much we eat and limit portions or make substitutions whenever possible.

• Substitute complex carbohydrates for foods high in saturated fat and cholesterol. Complex carbohydrate is another term for starch and fiber. Once thought of as fattening, starch now has gained new glory as a lowfat energy source. No need to skimp on pasta, cereals and rice. The potatoes we once shunned are now invited to our tables. Other sources of complex carbohydrates are breads, vegetables and fruits. Just go easy on the margarine, mayonnaise and creamy sauces.

LEARNING THE NUTRITION FACTS

Learning how to read labels will help you to make intelligent choices about the fat in foods you buy. Nutrition Facts is the revised nutrition label that food manufacturers are required by law to use in order to tell us the nutritional content of foods. The hope is that this improved label will be more meaningful to everyone and will enable us to make better food choices. This new label should start appearing on food packaging in 1994.

Nutrition Facts provides much of the same information as the former label with changes in layout and in the emphasis on certain nutrients we want to know more about, namely total fat, calories from fat, and total carbohydrate (fiber and sugar). Nutrition Facts is listed for a serving of the food by itself (as packaged), as in dry cereal, and also may be listed for the food plus an added ingredient, such as cereal plus skim milk, or as prepared, since so many foods require us to cook or add other ingredients before we eat them.

Information about specific nutrients is provided in grams or milligrams per serving as packaged; as prepared information it may be footnoted only. Percent Daily Value, listed for each nutrient, is a new measure of how a food stacks up when compared to an average diet of 2,000 calories per day and may be listed for the product as packaged and as prepared. Percent Daily Value replaces the former Percent U.S. RDA for vitamins A and C, calcium and iron.

The calories per gram for fat, carbohydrate and protein listed at the bottom of the label enable the reader to calculate the number of calories that come from each component.

NUTRITION FACTS

Serving Size 1 cup (35 g)
Servings Per Container 10

Amount Per Serving	Cereal	Cereal with ½ cup Skim Milk
Calories	130	170
Calories from Fat	0	0
	% Daily Value**	
Total Fat 0 g*	0%	0%
Saturated Fat 0 g	0%	0%
Cholesterol 0 mg	0%	0%
Sodium 200 mg	8%	11%
Total Carbohydrate 30 g	10%	12%
Dietary Fiber 4 g	16%	16%
Sugar 18 g		
Protein 3 g		

*Amount in Cereal. One-half cup skim milk contributes an additional 40 calories, 65 mg sodium, 6 g total carbohydrate (6 g sugars), and 4 g protein.
**Percent Daily Values are based on a 2,000-calorie diet. Your daily values may be higher or lower depending on your calorie needs:

	Calories:	2,000	2,500
Total Fat	Less than	65 g	80 g
Sat Fat	Less than	20 g	25 g
Cholesterol	Less than	300 mg	300 mg
Sodium	Less than	2,400 mg	2,400 mg
Total Carbohydrate		300 g	375 g
Dietary Fiber		25 g	30 g

Calories per gram:
Fat 9 · Carbohdyrate 4 · Protein 4

Amount Per Serving	Cereal	Cereal with ½ cup Skim Milk
Vitamin A	25%	25%
Vitamin C	25%	25%
Calcium	0%	15%
Iron	10%	10%

FOLLOWING THE FOOD GUIDE PYRAMID

The Food Guide Pyramid (below) is your guide to healthy food choices.

FOOD GUIDE PYRAMID: A Guide to Daily Food Choices

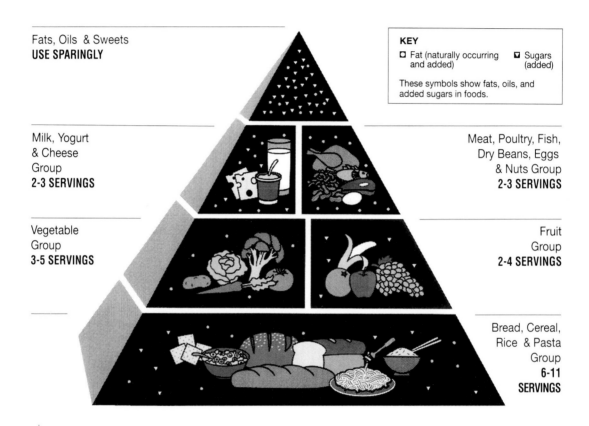

Fats, Oils & Sweets
USE SPARINGLY

KEY
▢ Fat (naturally occurring and added)   ☑ Sugars (added)

These symbols show fats, oils, and added sugars in foods.

Milk, Yogurt
& Cheese
Group
2-3 SERVINGS

Meat, Poultry, Fish,
Dry Beans, Eggs
& Nuts Group
2-3 SERVINGS

Vegetable
Group
3-5 SERVINGS

Fruit
Group
2-4 SERVINGS

Bread, Cereal,
Rice & Pasta
Group
**6-11
SERVINGS**

FAT CONTENT OF SELECTED FOODS

The following list will help you make sensible, low-fat food choices.

FOOD	MEASURE UNIT, WEIGHT	TOTAL FAT, G
Whole milk	1 cup	8.9
Skim milk	1 cup	0.4
Plain yogurt	6 ounces	5.5
Plain nonfat yogurt	6 ounces	0
Whipped heavy cream	2 tablespoons	1.3
Prepared whipped topping mix, prepared with whole milk	2 tablespoons	1.0
Vanilla ice cream, 16% fat	1 cup	23.7
Vanilla ice millk	1 cup	5.6

FOOD	MEASURE UNIT, WEIGHT	TOTAL FAT, G
Sour cream	1 cup	48.2
Lowfat sour cream	1 cup	28.8
Creamed cottage cheese	1 cup	9.5
Lowfat cottage cheese	1 cup	4.4
Ricotta cheese, whole milk	15 ounces	54.8
Lowfat ricotta cheese, skim	15 ounces	33.6
Cream cheese	1 ounce	9.9
Neufchâtel cheese	1 ounce	6.6
Cheddar cheese	1 ounce	9.0
Lowfat Cheddar cheese	1 ounce	5.0
Swiss cheese	1 ounce	8.0
Lowfat Swiss cheese	1 ounce	5.0
Lard	1 tablespoon	12.8
Butter	1 tablespoon	11.5
Margarine, corn	1 tablespoon	11.5
Reduced-calorie margarine	1 tablespoon	8.0
Eggs	1 large	5.1
Cholesterol-free egg product	¼ cup	0
Vegetable oil, corn	1 tablespoon	13.6
Nonstick cooking spray	1 spray	1.0
Mayonnaise, soybean	1 tablespoon	11.0
Cholesterol-free reduced-calorie mayonnaise	1 tablespoon	5.0
Italian salad dressing	1 tablespoon, bottled	8.0
Reduced-calorie Italian salad dressing	1 tablespoon, bottled	0
Blue cheese salad dressing	1 tablespoon, bottled	6.0
Reduced-calorie blue cheese salad dressing	1 tablespoon, bottled	2.0
Egg noodles	2 ounces, dry	3.0
Cholesterol-free noodles	2 ounces, dry	1.0
Tuna, oil packed, drained	3 ounces, canned	6.9
Tuna, water packed, drained	3 ounces, canned	2.1
Salmon, Chinook	3 ounces, baked	11.0
Flounder, sole	3 ounces, baked	1.3
Crab legs	3 ounces, cooked	1.0
Imitation crabmeat sticks	3 ounces, cooked	1.1
Ground beef	3 ounces, broiled	17.6
Extra-lean ground beef	3 ounces, broiled	13.9
Beef boneless rib roast	3 ounces, roasted	8.0
Beef top round steak	3 ounces, broiled	6.0
Pork shoulder blade steak	3 ounces, braised	14.0
Pork loin tenderloin	3 ounces, roasted	4.0
Chicken, dark meat without skin	3 ounces, roasted	8.3
Chicken, light meat without skin	3 ounces, roasted	3.8
Turkey, dark meat without skin	3 ounces, roasted	6.1

(continued)

FOOD	MEASURE UNIT, WEIGHT	TOTAL FAT, G
Turkey, white meat without skin	3 ounces, roasted	2.7
White layer cake with white frosting	1/12 slice	14.0
White angel food cake, unfrosted	1/12 slice	0

Sources: Compiled by General Mills, Inc., from U.S. Department of Agriculture Handbook #8. Michigan State University data base. Egg Board, produce labels and manufacturer information.

HOW TO USE NUTRITION INFORMATION

Nutrition Information per serving for each recipe includes the amounts of calories, protein, carbohydrate, fat, cholesterol and sodium.

- If ingredient choices are given, the first listed ingredient is used in recipe nutrition information calculations.

- When ingredient ranges or more than one serving size is indicated, the first weight or serving is used to calculate nutrition information.

- "If desired" ingredients and recipe variations are not included in nutrition information calculations.

Menus

Company Dinner
Mushroom Rounds (page 18)
Chicken Breasts with Sun-dried–Tomato Sauce
  (page 45)
Caesar Salad with Low-Fat Dressing
Chocolate Swirl Cheesecake with Raspberry
  Topping (page 83)
Wine or Sparkling Water

Easy Workday Dinner
Oriental Barbecued Chicken (page 43)
Coleslaw
Prepared Cornbread
Fresh Fruit
Skim Milk

Meatless Dinner
Hearty Bean and Pasta Stew (page 58)
Crusty French Bread
Fresh Blueberry Cobbler (page 81)
Apple Cider

Catch of the Day
Poached Fish Dijon (page 23)
Steamed Green Beans
Spanish Rice
Gingerbread with Orange Sauce (page 85)

Mexican Night
Fresh Tomato Salsa (page 14)
Spicy Tortilla Chips (page 19)
Extra-Easy Beef Fajitas (page 65)
Creamy Peach Freeze (page 79)
Hot Chocolate

Relaxing Brunch
Spinach Frittata with Creole Sauce (page 51)
Bran Muffins with Spreadable Fruit
Spicy Fruit Compote (page 79)
Coconut-Almond Macaroons (page 89)

Green Herb Dip

1

Tasty Appetizers

Green Herb Dip

¾ cup plain lowfat yogurt
¼ cup cholesterol-free reduced-calorie
  mayonnaise or salad dressing
¼ teaspoon salt
½ cup watercress leaves
½ cup fresh parsley leaves
¼ cup fresh basil leaves
1 green onion, cut into 1-inch pieces

Place yogurt, mayonnaise and salt in blender or food processor. Add remaining ingredients. Cover and blend, or process, about 30 seconds, stopping blender occasionally to scrape sides, until finely chopped. Cover and refrigerate about 1 hour or until slightly thickened and chilled. Serve with raw vegetables if desired.

About 1 cup

PER TABLESPOON: Calories 20; Protein 1 g; Carbohydrate 1 g; Fat 1 g; Cholesterol 0 mg; Sodium 75 mg

Eggplant Dip

For an extra flavor boost, stir in a few tablespoons of plain yogurt or sesame seed paste.

1 small eggplant (about 1 pound)
1 small onion, cut into fourths
1 clove garlic
¼ cup lemon juice
1 tablespoon olive or vegetable oil
1 teaspoon salt
Assorted raw vegetables

Heat oven to 400°. Prick eggplant 3 or 4 times with fork. Bake about 40 minutes or until tender; cool. Peel eggplant; cut into cubes. Place eggplant, onion, garlic, lemon juice, oil and salt in blender. Cover and blend on high speed until smooth. Serve with vegetables.

About 2 cups

PER TABLESPOON: Calories 10; Protein 0 g; Carbohydrate 1 g; Fat g; Cholesterol 0 mg; Sodium 70 mg

Fresh Tomato Salsa

This fresh, fat-free dip adds excitement to everything it touches. Try it with taco chips, fish, eggs and meat.

½ cup sliced green onions
½ cup chopped green bell pepper
2 to 3 tablespoons lime juice
2 tablespoons chopped cilantro
1 tablespoon finely chopped jalapeño chiles
½ teaspoon salt
3 medium tomatoes, seeded and chopped (about 3 cups)
3 cloves garlic, finely chopped

Mix all ingredients. Serve with tortilla chips, crackers or vegetables if desired.

About 3½ cups

PER TABLESPOON: Calories 2; Protein 0 g; Carbohydrate 1 g; Fat 0 g; Cholesterol 0 mg; Sodium 10 mg

Black Bean Dip

Make your own low-fat chips easily from pita breads: Heat oven to 400°. Cut around outside edges of pita breads to separate layers. Cut each layer into 8 wedges. Place wedges on ungreased cookie sheet. Bake 8 to 10 minutes or until light brown and crisp.

1 tablespoon chopped green chiles
¼ cup chopped onion (about 1 small)
1 clove garlic, crushed
1 can (15 ounces) black beans, drained
½ cup plain nonfat yogurt
½ teaspoon ground cumin
¼ teaspoon salt

Place chiles, onion, garlic and beans in blender or food processor. Cover and blend, or process, until almost smooth. Stir in yogurt, cumin and salt. Serve cold, or heat in 1½-quart saucepan over medium heat, stirring frequently, until hot. Serve with chips or crackers.

About 2 cups

MICROWAVE DIRECTIONS: Place dip in 1½-quart microwavable casserole. Microwave uncovered on high 3 to 4 minutes, stirring every minute, until hot.

PER TABLESPOON; Calories 10; Protein 1 g; Carbohydrate 2 g; Fat 0 g; Cholesterol 0 mg; Sodium 55 mg

Snack Tips

- Use fruits and vegetables (steamed or uncooked) in place of chips and crackers.

- Make your own chips to save on fat and calories. Toast thin bagel slices and pita bread wedges.

- Always read the labels on commercial cracker and snack products. When choosing purchases, look for items without animal fats (lard or tallow) or saturated fats.

- Substitute lowfat or nonfat yogurt for sour cream or mayonnaise in your favorite recipes for dips and spreads. Reduced-calorie mayonnaise or salad dressing is a step in the right direction, but substitute some lowfat or nonfat yogurt for part of it.

- Don't forget that herbs and spices give wonderful flavor to dips and spreads— without adding salt, as dry mixes can.

Bell Pepper Spread

¾ **cup finely chopped red bell pepper (about 1 medium)**
¾ **cup finely chopped yellow bell pepper (about 1 medium)**
½ **cup part-skim ricotta cheese**
¼ **cup chopped parsley**
2 **tablespoons chopped fresh or 2 teaspoons dried basil leaves**
4 **drops red pepper sauce**
½ **package (8-ounce size) Neufchâtel cheese**

Mix all ingredients in medium bowl. Serve with Spicy Tortilla Chips (page 19) or crackers if desired.   **About 2 cups**

PER TABLESPOON: Calories 15; Protein 1 g; Carbohydrate 1 g; Fat 1 g; Cholesterol 5 mg; Sodium 20 mg

Chutney-glazed Yogurt Spread

Thick Yogurt is very versatile. It is also used in Chocolate Swirl Cheesecake with Raspberry Topping (page 83).

Thick Yogurt (right)
½ **cup shredded low-fat Cheddar cheese (2 ounces)**
1 **tablespoon finely chopped green onion**
½ **teaspoon curry powder**
1 **jar (9 ounces) chutney (about 1 cup)**
2 **tablespoons chopped green onions**

Prepare Thick Yogurt. Mix yogurt, cheese, 1 tablespoon onion and the curry powder. Spread mixture about ¾ inch thick in shallow 8-inch serving dish. Top with chutney. Sprinkle with 2 tablespoons onions. Serve with plain toast rounds or crackers if desired.

About 2 cups

Thick Yogurt

Line 6-inch strainer with basket-style paper coffee filter or double-thickness cheesecloth. Place strainer over bowl. Spoon 4 cups plain nonfat yogurt into strainer. Cover strainer and bowl and refrigerate at least 12 hours, draining liquid from bowl occasionally.

PER TABLESPOON: Calories 35; Protein 2 g; Carbohydrate 5 g; Fat 0 g; Cholesterol 0 mg; Sodium 45 mg

Herbed Yogurt Cheese

Homemade yogurt cheese, with half the calories of rich cream cheese, has the same smooth texture. It is delicious and versatile even without the dill weed and garlic. You can pack the cheese into a heart-shaped coeur à la crème mold rather than a strainer. Because these molds have fewer drainage holes, refrigerate the cheese six hours longer.

4 **cups nonfat plain yogurt**
¼ **cup chopped fresh or 1 tablespoon dried dill weed**
1 **teaspoon salt**
2 **cloves garlic, finely chopped**

Line 6-inch strainer with basket-style paper coffee filter or double thickness cheesecloth. Place strainer over bowl. Mix all ingredients; pour into strainer. Cover strainer and bowl; refrigerate at least 12 hours, draining liquid from bowl occasionally. Unmold onto plate. Garnish with freshly ground pepper and additional dill weed if desired.   **About 1¼ cups**

PER TABLESPOON: Calories 25; Protein 2 g; Carbohydrate 3 g; Fat 0 g; Cholesterol 0 mg; Sodium 140 mg

Salsa Verde, Spicy Tortilla Chips (page 19)

Fruit and Yogurt Dip

1 cup vanilla yogurt
¼ cup flaked coconut, toasted if desired
2 tablespoons packed brown sugar
1 can (8 ounces) crushed pineapple in
   juice, drained

Mix all ingredients. Cover and refrigerate at least 1 hour. Serve with fresh fruit or cheese cubes if desired. **About 2 cups**

PER TABLESPOON: Calories 15; Protein 0 g; Carbohydrate 2 g; Fat 0 g; Cholesterol 0 mg; Sodium 5 mg

Salsa Verde

Tomatillos are the basis of Mexican and Southwestern green sauces and salsas. Look for bright green tomatillos with their husks drawn tightly around them. After husking, rinse well to remove the sticky residue.

¼ cup chopped onion (about 1 small)
2 tablespoons lightly packed cilantro
2 tablespoons lightly packed watercress
1 teaspoon vegetable oil
¼ teaspoon salt
8 ounces tomatillos, cut in half
1 to 2 small green chiles, seeded

Place all ingredients in blender or food processor. Cover and blend, or process, until smooth. Cover and refrigerate any remaining salsa.
About 1 cup

PER TABLESPOON: Calories 10; Protein 0 g; Carbohydrate 1 g; Fat 0 g; Cholesterol 0 mg; Sodium 35 mg

Spicy Carrots and Jicama

Jicama is becoming widely available. This large, scrubby root looks rather like a turnip and has the juicy crunch of water chestnut.

¼ cup lemon juice
2 teaspoons vegetable oil
½ teaspoon garlic powder
½ teaspoon chile powder
⅛ to ¼ teaspoon ground red pepper
   (cayenne)
4 medium carrots (about ½ pound)
½ pound jicama

Shake all ingredients except carrots and jicama in tightly covered container. Cut carrots lengthwise into fourths; cut each fourth crosswise into halves. Pare jicama; cut into 3 × ¼ × ¼-inch strips. Place vegetables in glass or plastic bowl or in heavy plastic bag. Pour lemon juice mixture over vegetables; toss well. Cover and refrigerate at least 2 hours, stirring occasionally. Drain before serving. **About 80 appetizers**

PER APPETIZER: Calories 5; Protein 0 g; Carbohydrate 1 g; Fat 0 g; Cholesterol 0 mg; Sodium 2 mg

Cucumber Wedges

2 medium cucumbers
1 tablespoon lime juice
1 teaspoon coarse salt
½ teaspoon chile powder

Cut cucumbers lengthwise into fourths; cut fourths into 2-inch pieces. Place in single layer on serving plate. Drizzle with lime juice. Sprinkle with salt and chile powder.

About 30 appetizers

PER APPETIZER: Calories 2; Protein 0 g; Carbohydrate 1 g; Fat 0 g; Cholesterol 0 mg; Sodium 75 mg

Mushroom Rounds

1 tablespoon margarine
1 cup very finely chopped mushrooms
(about 7 medium)
½ teaspoon chopped fresh or ⅛ tea-
spoon dried thyme leaves
½ teaspoon salt
Eighteen 1½-inch melba toast rounds

Heat margarine in 10-inch nonstick skillet until melted. Cook mushrooms and thyme in margarine over low heat, stirring frequently, until mushrooms are tender. Stir in salt. Spread about ½ teaspoon mushroom mixture on each toast round. Serve immediately.   **6 servings**

PER   SERVING: Calories 65;   Protein 2 g;   Carbohydrate 9 g; Fat 2 g; Cholesterol 0 mg; Sodium 310 mg

Stuffed Pattypan Squash

16 tiny pattypan squash (about 1½
inches in diameter)*
½ cup soft bread crumbs (about ¾ slice
bread)
1 teaspoon chopped fresh or ¼ teaspoon
dried thyme leaves
¼ teaspoon salt
2 green onions, finely chopped
1 tablespoon grated Parmesan cheese

Heat oven to 350°. Heat 1 inch water to boiling. Add squash. Cook 6 to 8 minutes or until crisp-tender; drain. Cut off stem ends. Hollow out squash; reserve squash shells. Chop squash meat finely. Mix squash and remaining ingredients except cheese. Spoon 1 heaping teaspoon filling into each squash shell. Sprinkle with

8 small pattypan squash (about 2½ inches in diameter) can be substituted for the tiny squash. Spoon 1 heaping tablespoon filling into each squash shell.

cheese. Place in ungreased square pan, 9 × 9 × 2 inches. Bake uncovered 10 to 12 minutes or until hot.   **8 servings**

MICROWAVE DIRECTIONS: Place squash and 2 tablespoons water in square microwavable dish, 8 × 8 × 2 inches. Cover tightly and microwave on high 3 to 5 minutes or until crisp-tender; drain. Hollow out and fill squash shells as directed. Place in square dish. Cover tightly and microwave 2 to 3 minutes or until hot.

PER   SERVING: Calories 15;   Protein 1 g;   Carbohydrate 3 g; Fat 0 g; Cholesterol 0 mg; Sodium 95 mg

Melon and Prosciutto

Prosciutto is a type of Italian ham cured by a special drying process, usually sold very thinly sliced.

1 large cantaloupe, casaba, honeydew or
Spanish melon (about 3 pounds)
¼ pound thinly sliced prosciutto,* cut
into 1-inch strips

Cut melon in half. Scoop out seeds and fibers. Cut each half lengthwise into 6 wedges and remove rind. Cut crosswise slits 1½ inches apart in each melon wedge. Place several strips of prosciutto over each wedge. Push prosciutto into slits using blade of table knife.

          12 servings

¼ pound thinly sliced ham can be substituted for the prosciutto.

MELON AND PROSCIUTTO BITES: Cut each melon wedge into 6 pieces. Wrap each piece in strips of prosciutto. Secure with wooden picks.

PER   SERVING: Calories 25;   Protein 2 g;   Carbohydrate 3 g; Fat 1 g; Cholesterol 2 mg; Sodium 110 mg

Mushroom Pita Pizzas

2 pita breads (6 inches in diameter)
2 cups sliced mushrooms*
1 small red onion, thinly sliced and separated into rings
¼ cup chopped green bell pepper
2 tablespoons chopped fresh or 2 teaspoons dried basil leaves
1 cup finely shredded mozzarella cheese (4 ounces)
1 tablespoon grated Parmesan cheese

Heat oven to 425°. Split each bread into halves around edge with knife to make 4 rounds. Place rounds, cut sides up, on ungreased cookie sheet. Arrange mushrooms on bread rounds. Top with onion rings and bell pepper; sprinkle with basil and cheeses. Bake until cheese is melted, 8 to 10 minutes. Cut each round into 8 pieces. **8 servings**

*1 can (4 ounces) mushroom stems and pieces, drained, can be substituted for fresh mushrooms.

PER SERVING: Calories 90; Protein 6 g; Carbohydrate 10 g; Fat 3 g; Cholesterol 8 mg; Sodium 80 mg

Spicy Tortilla Chips

2 tablespoons margarine, melted
½ teaspoon chile powder
8 corn or flour tortillas (8 inches in diameter)

Heat oven to 400°. Mix margarine and chile powder; brush on one side of tortillas. Cut each into 12 wedges. Place on ungreased jelly roll pan, 15½ × 10½ × 1 inch. Bake uncovered 8 to 10 minutes or until crisp and golden brown; cool. (Tortillas will continue to crisp as they cool.) **96 chips**

PER CHIP: Calories 10; Protein 0 g; Carbohydrate 1 g; Fat 0 g; Cholesterol 0 mg; Sodium 3 mg

Shopping Tips

- Plan meals and make a grocery list. Stick to your list.

- Don't shop when you're hungry. Eat something nutritious, such as a banana or slice of whole-grain bread before you go shopping. Extra items have a way of sneaking into your cart when you are feeling hungry.

- Read food labels. Be sure you understand the label terminology. For example, "reduced-fat" does not necessarily mean that a product is low in fat; it's just that the food has less fat than the original product. New food labeling regulations are designed to clear up confusion about different terms. See Learning the Nutrition Facts on page 6.

- When buying meat, look for lean cuts such as rounds and tenderloins. Many cuts of meat are now labeled with percentages of fat to help you choose the fat content you want.

- Purchase turkeys that are not self-basting. Select ground turkey breast or ground turkey labeled *lean;* if not so labeled, it may not be low in fat.

- Buy water-packed canned fish products, such as water-packed tuna or salmon, instead of products packed in oil.

- Select skim, nonfat, or low-fat dairy products such as milk, yogurt, cheese and sour cream. Many of the new products on the market taste as good—or better—than the original!

Chinese Firecrackers, Stuffed Pattypan Squash (page 18)

Chinese Firecrackers

Twisted in a crisp phyllo wrapping, these sweet-and-sour appetizers look like little firecrackers.

  1 teaspoon vegetable oil
  ½ pound ground turkey
  1 cup finely chopped cabbage
  ½ cup shredded carrot (about 1 medium)
  2 tablespoons finely chopped green onions
  1 tablespoon chile paste or puree
  1 tablespoon dry white wine or chicken broth
  1 teaspoon cornstarch
  14 frozen phyllo leaves (13 × 9 inches), thawed
  1 tablespoon plus 1 teaspoon vegetable oil
  ¾ cup sweet-and-sour sauce

Heat 1 teaspoon oil in 10-inch nonstick skillet. Cook ground turkey, cabbage, carrot and onions in oil over medium heat about 5 minutes, stirring frequently, until turkey is done and vegetables are crisp-tender. Stir in chile paste. Mix wine and cornstarch; stir into turkey mixture. Cook uncovered, stirring occasionally, until slightly thickened.

Heat oven to 375°. Cut phyllo leaves crosswise in half. Cover with damp towel to keep from drying out. Place 1 piece phyllo on flat surface. Brush with small amount of oil. Top with second piece phyllo. Place about 2 tablespoons turkey mixture on short end of phyllo; shape into about 4-inch log. Roll up phyllo and turkey mixture. Twist phyllo 1 inch from each end to form firecracker shape. Repeat with remaining phyllo and turkey mixture. Brush firecrackers with remaining oil.

Bake on ungreased cookie sheet 18 to 22 minutes or until phyllo is crisp and golden brown. Serve with sweet-and-sour sauce.

14 appetizers

PER APPETIZER; Calories 190; Protein 7 g; Carbohydrate 35 g; Fat 3 g; Cholesterol 10 mg; Sodium 210 mg

Potato Snacks

Here is the wonderful flavor of French fried potatoes without all the fat. These homemade chips recall the famous Saratoga chips of days gone by.

  3 medium unpared potatoes (about 1 pound)
  Vegetable oil
  1 teaspoon salt
  ½ teaspoon sugar
  ½ teaspoon paprika
  ¼ teaspoon dry mustard
  ⅛ teaspoon garlic powder

Set oven control to broil. Cut potatoes lengthwise into eighths. Place potatoes, cut sides down, in ungreased jelly roll pan, 15½ × 10½ × 1 inch. Brush lightly with oil. Mix remaining ingredients; sprinkle potatoes with half of the mixture. Broil potatoes with tops about 3 inches from heat until they bubble slightly, about 10 minutes. Turn; brush with oil and sprinkle with remaining salt mixture. Broil until golden brown and tender, about 5 minutes longer. Serve with reduced-calorie sour cream if desired.

6 servings

PER SERVING: Calories 80; Protein 2 g; Carbohydrate 14 g; Fat 2 g; Cholesterol 0 mg; Sodium 370 mg

Seafood Stew with Rosmarina (page 38)

2

Fish and Shellfish

Poached Fish Dijon

Milk added to the flavorful poaching liquid keeps white fish snowy white.

1 pound cod or firm lean fish fillets
2 cups water
⅓ cup skim milk
½ teaspoon salt
1 lemon, peeled, thinly sliced and seeded
Dijon-Dill Sauce (right)

If fish fillets are large, cut into 4 serving pieces. Heat water, milk, salt and lemon slices to boiling in 10-inch skillet. Place fish in skillet. Heat to boiling; reduce heat. Simmer uncovered until fish flakes easily with fork, 8 to 10 minutes.

Prepare Dijon-Dill Sauce. Remove fish with slotted spatula; drain. Serve fish with sauce.

4 servings

Dijon-Dill Sauce

⅔ cup skim milk
1 tablespoon Dijon mustard
2 teaspoons cornstarch
1½ teaspoons chopped fresh or ½ teaspoon dried dill weed
⅛ teaspoon salt

Heat all ingredients to boiling over medium heat, stirring constantly. Boil and stir 1 minute.

MICROWAVE DIRECTIONS: Mix 1 cup hot water, the milk, salt and lemon slices in square microwavable dish, 8 × 8 × 2 inches. Cover with vented plastic wrap and microwave on high to boiling. Add fish with thickest parts to outside edges. Cover and microwave until fish flakes easily with fork, 5 to 7 minutes.

Mix all ingredients for Dijon-Dill Sauce in 2-cup microwavable measure. Microwave uncovered on high, stirring every minute, until thickened, 2 to 3 minutes.

PER SERVING: Calories 140; Protein 21 g; Carbohydrate 5 g; Fat 4 g; Cholesterol 40 mg; Sodium 530 mg

Salsa Fish

Cilantro, a southwestern favorite, is also known as fresh coriander, Mexican parsley and Chinese parsley. While cilantro resembles flat-leaf parsley, its flavor is more intense.

    1 pound cod, orange roughy or other
        medium-fat fish fillets (about ½ inch
        thick)
    1 cup chopped tomato (about 1 large)
    ½ cup chopped green bell pepper (about
        1 small)
    ¼ cup chopped onion (about 1 small)
    2 tablespoons finely chopped cilantro or
        parsley
    ¼ teaspoon salt
    ¼ cup dry white wine or chicken broth

If fish fillets are large, cut into 4 serving pieces. Spray 10-inch nonstick skillet with nonstick cooking spray. Heat over medium heat. Arrange fish in single layer in skillet. Cook uncovered 4 to 6 minutes, turning once, until fish flakes easily with fork. Remove fish to warm platter; keep warm.

Cook remaining ingredients except wine in skillet over medium heat 3 to 5 minutes, stirring frequently, until bell pepper and onion are crisp-tender. Stir in wine. Heat until hot. Spoon tomato mixture over fish.   **4 servings**

PER SERVING: Calories 150; Protein 24 g; Carbohydrate 6 g; Fat 2 g; Cholesterol 40 mg; Sodium 210 mg

Oriental Fish with Bok Choy

    1 pound orange roughy or other lean fish
        fillets
    ½ pound bok choy
    1 tablespoon sesame seed
    1 tablespoon vegetable oil
    1 bunch green onions, cut into 2-inch
        pieces
    1 small red bell pepper, cut into 1-inch
        pieces
    ½ cup chicken broth
    ½ teaspoon red pepper flakes
    1 tablespoon cornstarch
    1 tablespoon teriyaki sauce
    2 cups hot cooked rice

Cut fish fillets into 1-inch pieces. Remove leaves from bok choy. Cut leaves into ½-inch strips and stems into ¼-inch slices. Cook sesame seed in oil in 10-inch skillet over medium heat, stirring occasionally, until golden brown. Add bok choy stems, onions, bell pepper, fish, broth and pepper flakes. Heat to boiling; reduce heat. Cover and simmer about 5 minutes or until fish flakes easily with fork.

Mix cornstarch and teriyaki sauce. Gradually stir into fish mixture. Heat to boiling, stirring constantly. Boil and stir 1 minute. Stir in bok choy leaves and heat until wilted. Serve over rice.   **4 servings**

PER SERVING: Calories 280; Protein 24 g; Carbohydrate 31 g; Fat 7 g; Cholesterol 30 mg; Sodium 650 mg

Sweet-and-Sour Fish

A low-fat version of an Oriental favorite!

1 can (8 ounces) pineapple chunks in juice, drained (reserve juice)
3 tablespoons sugar
¼ cup vinegar
1 teaspoon soy sauce
¼ teaspoon salt
1 small clove garlic, finely chopped
2 tablespoons cornstarch
2 tablespoons cold water
1 small green bell pepper, cut into ½-inch strips
1 pound lean fish steaks, ½ to ¾ inch thick
¼ teaspoon salt
1 tomato, cut into 8 wedges

Heat oven to 350°. Add enough water to pineapple juice to measure 1 cup. Heat pineapple juice, sugar, vinegar, soy sauce, ¼ teaspoon salt and the garlic to boiling in 2-quart saucepan. Mix cornstarch and water; stir into sauce. Boil and stir 1 minute. Stir in pineapple chunks and bell pepper.

Place fish steaks in ungreased square baking dish, 8 × 8 × 2 inches; sprinkle with ¼ teaspoon salt. Pour pineapple mixture over fish. Bake uncovered until fish flakes easily with fork, 25 to 30 minutes. Add tomato wedges during the last 5 minutes of cooking. **4 servings**

PER SERVING: Calories 210; Protein 20 g; Carbohydrate 24 g; Fat 4 g; Cholesterol 35 mg; Sodium 470 mg

Easy Fish and Vegetable Packets

4 frozen lean fish fillets (about 1 pound)
1 package (16 ounces) frozen broccoli, cauliflower and carrots
1 tablespoon chopped fresh or 1 teaspoon dried dill weed
½ teaspoon salt
¼ teaspoon pepper
4 tablespoons dry white wine or chicken broth

Heat oven to 450°. Place each frozen fish fillet on 12-inch square of aluminum foil. Top each fish fillet with one-fourth of the vegetables; sprinkle with dill weed, salt and pepper. Pour 1 tablespoon wine over each. Fold up sides of foil to make tent; fold top edges over to seal. Fold in sides, making a packet; fold to seal. Place packets on cookie sheet. Bake about 40 minutes or until vegetables are crisp-tender and fish flakes easily with fork. **4 servings**

PER SERVING: Calories 160; Protein 25 g; Carbohydrate 7 g; Fat 2 g; Cholesterol 40 mg; Sodium 380 mg

Savory Fish en Papillote

Savory Fish en Papillote

1 pound orange roughy or other lean fish fillets
4 twelve-inch circles cooking parchment paper
4 teaspoons chopped fresh or 1 teaspoon dried oregano leaves
¼ teaspoon salt
⅛ teaspoon pepper
1 small onion, thinly sliced
1 small tomato, thinly sliced
1 small zucchini, thinly sliced
¼ cup sliced ripe olives

Heat oven to 400°. Cut fish fillets into 4 serving pieces. Place each piece fish on half of each parchment circle. Sprinkle fish with oregano, salt and pepper. Layer onion, tomato, zucchini and olives on fish. Fold other half of circle over fish and vegetables. Beginning at one end, seal edge by turning up and folding tightly 2 or 3 times. Twist each end several times to secure. Place on ungreased cookie sheet.

Bake 20 to 25 minutes or until vegetables are crisp-tender and fish flakes easily with fork. To serve, cut a large X on top of each packet; fold back points.   **4 servings**

MICROWAVE DIRECTIONS: Prepare and wrap fish fillets and vegetables as directed. Arrange packets in circle in microwave oven. Microwave on high 7 to 8 minutes, rearranging packet after 4 minutes, until vegetables are crisp-tender and fish flakes easily with fork. Let stand 3 minutes before cutting X in packets.

PER SERVING: Calories 160; Protein 25 g; Carbohydrate 5 g; Fat 4 g; Cholesterol 35 mg; Sodium 260 mg

Halibut Stir-fry

Sesame oil with its high smoking point is perfect for a stir-fry. We suggest using darker, Oriental sesame oil in this recipe as it has a more robust flavor than light sesame oil.

2 teaspoons sesame oil
1 pound halibut or other lean fish steaks, cut into 1-inch pieces
1 medium onion, thinly sliced
3 cloves garlic, finely chopped
1 teaspoon finely chopped gingerroot
1 package (10 ounces) frozen asparagus cuts, thawed and drained
1 cup sliced mushrooms or 1 can (4 ounces) sliced mushrooms, drained
2 tablespoons soy sauce
1 tablespoon lemon juice
1 medium tomato, cut into thin wedges

Heat oil in 10-inch nonstick skillet over medium-high heat. Add fish, onion, garlic, gingerroot and asparagus; stir-fry 2 to 3 minutes or until fish almost flakes with fork. Carefully stir in remaining ingredients; heat thoroughly. Serve with additional soy sauce if desired.   **4 servings**

PER SERVING: Calories 195; Protein 27 g; Carbohydrate 10 g; Fat 5 g; Cholesterol 35 mg; Sodium 730 mg

Vegetable-stuffed Sole

½ teaspoon salt
1 teaspoon chopped fresh or ½ teaspoon dried dill weed
¼ teaspoon pepper
6 sole or other lean fish fillets (about 2 pounds)
2 medium carrots, cut into julienne strips
1 green bell pepper, cut into julienne strips
¼ cup dry white wine or apple juice
2 tablespoons margarine or butter
2 tablespoons all-purpose flour
½ teaspoon salt
⅛ teaspoon pepper
1 cup milk
¼ cup dry white wine or apple juice

Heat oven to 350°. Mix ½ teaspoon salt, the dill weed and ¼ teaspoon pepper. Sprinkle over fish fillets. Divide carrot and bell pepper strips among fish. Roll up fish and place seam sides down in ungreased rectangular baking dish, 13 × 9 × 2 inches. Pour ¼ cup wine over fish. Cover with aluminum foil and bake about 40 minutes or until fish flakes easily with fork.

Heat margarine in 1½-quart saucepan until melted. Stir in flour, ½ teaspoon salt and ⅛ teaspoon pepper. Cook over medium heat, stirring constantly, until smooth and bubbly; remove from heat. Stir in milk and ¼ cup wine. Heat to boiling, stirring constantly. Boil and stir 1 minute.

Arrange fish on serving platter. Pour sauce over fish. Garnish with dill weed if desired.

6 servings

MICROWAVE DIRECTIONS: Place carrot strips in rectangular microwavable dish, 11 × 7 × 1½ inches. Add 1 tablespoon wine. Cover tightly and microwave on high about 4 minutes or until crisp-tender. Remove with slotted spoon. Prepare fish fillets as directed. Arrange seam sides down around sides of dish. Drizzle with 3 tablespoons wine. Cover tightly and microwave on high 10 to 12 minutes, rotating dish one-half turn after 5 minutes, until fish flakes easily with fork. Let stand covered 3 minutes. Remove to warm platter and keep warm.

Microwave margarine in 4-cup microwavable measure uncovered on high 15 to 30 seconds or until melted. Stir in flour, ½ teaspoon salt and ⅛ teaspoon pepper. Gradually stir in milk and ¼ cup wine. Microwave uncovered on high about 4 minutes, stirring every minute, until thickened.

PER SERVING: Calories 225; Protein 28 g; Carbohydrate 10 g; Fat 6 g; Cholesterol 45 mg; Sodium 440 mg

Fat Content of Fish

Lean Fish Less Than 2.5 Fat	Medium-Fat Fish 2.5–5% Fat	Fatty Fish More Than 5% Fat
Cod	Anchovy	Butterfish
Haddock	Bluefish	Herring
Halibut	Catfish	Mackerel:
Grouper	Croaker	Atlantic,
Mackerel:	Mullet	Pacific,
King	Porgy	Spanish
Mahimahi	Redfish	Pompano
Ocean Perch	Salmon: Pink	Sablefish
Orange	Shark	Salmon:
Roughy	Swordfish	Chinook,
Pike	Trout:	Coho,
Red Snapper	Rainbow,	Sockeye
Sole	Sea	Sardine
Striped Bass	Tuna: Bluefin	Shad
Tuna:	Whitefish	Tuna:
Skipjack,		Albacore
Yellowfin		Trout: Lake

Source: Compiled by General Mills, Inc., from National Fisheries Institute, 1990.

Apple-Stuffed Sole

4 Dover sole or other thin lean fish fillets (about 1 pound)
¼ teaspoon salt
¼ teaspoon pepper
4 cups ¼-inch slices unpeeled cooking apples (about 3 medium)
1 green onion, cut lengthwise into fourths and crosswise into 3-inch pieces
½ cup unsweetened apple juice
¼ cup chopped green onions
½ teaspoon ground cinnamon
¼ cup reduced-calorie sour cream

Heat oven to 350°. Sprinkle fish fillets with salt and pepper. Place 3 apple slices in the center of each fillet; top with onion pieces. Fold fillets into thirds.

Mix remaining apples, the apple juice, chopped onions and cinnamon. Spoon into ungreased square baking dish, 8 × 8 × 2 inches. Arrange fillets, seam sides down, over apples. Cover and bake 35 to 45 minutes or until fish flakes easily with fork and apples are tender. Stir enough drippings into sour cream until of desired consistency; serve with fish. Sprinkle with ground cinnamon if desired. **4 servings**

PER SERVING: Calories 240; Protein 22 g; Carbohydrate 23 g; Fat 7 g; Cholesterol 65 mg; Sodium 180 mg

Zesty Red Snapper with Mushrooms

½ teaspoon paprika
1½ teaspoons chopped fresh or ½ teaspoon dried tarragon leaves
1½ teaspoons chopped fresh or ½ teaspoon dried oregano leaves
½ teaspoon salt
⅛ teaspoon pepper
⅛ teaspoon ground red pepper (cayenne)
1 pound red snapper or lean fish fillets
2 tablespoons lemon juice
1 cup sliced mushrooms

Heat oven to 400°. Mix paprika, tarragon, oregano, salt, pepper and red pepper. If fish fillets are large, cut into 4 serving pieces. Brush with 1 tablespoon of the lemon juice. Rub both sides of fish with herb mixture; arrange in ungreased rectangular baking dish, 12 × 7½ × 2 inches.

Cook and stir mushrooms in remaining lemon juice in 10-inch nonstick skillet over medium heat, about 2 minutes. Place mushrooms over fish. Cover and bake until fish flakes easily with fork, 15 to 20 minutes. **4 servings**

PER SERVING: Calories 120; Protein 19 g; Carbohydrate 2 g; Fat 4 g; Cholesterol 35 mg; Sodium 380 mg

Swordfish with Thyme-Apple Sauce

Swordfish with Thyme-Apple Sauce

Swordfish has a wonderful meaty quality that is very satisfying. Fresh thyme scents a sauce with apple slices.

Thyme-Apple Sauce (below)
1 pound swordfish or lean fish steaks,
  ½ to ¾ inch thick
2 tablespoons lemon juice

Prepare Thyme-Apple Sauce; keep warm.

Set oven control to broil. Place fish steaks on rack sprayed with nonstick cooking spray in broiler pan; brush with 1 tablespoon lemon juice. Broil with tops about 4 inches from heat 3 minutes. Turn; brush with remaining lemon juice. Broil until fish flakes easily with fork, 3 to 5 minutes longer. Serve with Thyme-Apple Sauce. **4 servings**

Thyme-Apple Sauce

2 tablespoons chopped onion
1 teaspoon vegetable oil
½ cup unsweetened apple juice
¼ cup water
1 tablespoon chopped fresh or ½ to 1
  teaspoon dried thyme leaves
1½ teaspoons cornstarch
¼ teaspoon salt
Coarsely ground pepper
1 large unpeeled red eating apple, thinly
  sliced

Cook and stir onion in oil in 2-quart nonstick saucepan over medium heat until onion is softened. Mix remaining ingredients except apple slices; stir into onion. Heat to boiling, stirring constantly. Boil and stir 1 minute. Stir in apple slices; heat until hot.

PER SERVING: Calories 170; Protein 19 g; Carbohydrate 13 g; Fat 5 g; Cholesterol 35 mg; Sodium 240 mg

Creole Catfish

This Southern dish is nice with corn bread and coleslaw.

2 pounds catfish or other medium-fat
  fish fillets
⅓ cup chopped green bell pepper
2 tablespoons chopped fresh parsley
1 tablespoon lemon juice
½ teaspoon salt
½ teaspoon ground red pepper (cayenne)
1 medium onion, chopped (about ½ cup)
1 clove garlic, crushed
1 can (28 ounces) whole tomatoes,
  undrained
3 cups hot cooked rice

Heat oven to 450°. If fillets are large, cut into 8 serving pieces. Place in ungreased rectangular baking dish, 11 × 7 × 1½ inches. Mix remaining ingredients except rice; break up tomatoes. Pour over fish.

Bake uncovered 25 to 30 minutes, spooning tomato mixture over fish occasionally, until fish flakes easily with fork. Serve over rice. Garnish with lemon slices sprinkled with chopped parsley if desired. **8 servings**

PER SERVING: Calories 220; Protein 21 g; Carbohydrate 25 g; Fat 4 g; Cholesterol 35 mg; Sodium 690 mg

Salmon with Cucumber Sauce

½ pound salmon fillets or other fatty fish fillets*
1 cup plain nonfat yogurt
1 tablespoon all-purpose flour
1 tablespoon chopped fresh or 1 teaspoon dried dill weed
1 teaspoon prepared horseradish
1 cup chopped seeded unpeeled cucumber (about 1 medium)
1 cup uncooked medium shell (conchiglie) or seashell macaroni (about 4 ounces)

Place salmon fillets in 2-quart saucepan; add enough water to cover. Heat to boiling; reduce heat. Simmer uncovered 6 to 8 minutes or until fish flakes easily with fork. Remove fish with slotted spatula; drain. Remove any skin. Flake fish into bite-size pieces; keep warm.

Mix yogurt and flour in same 2-quart saucepan. Stir in dill weed and horseradish. Heat over low heat until hot (do not boil). Stir in cucumber and fish. Cook macaroni as directed on package; drain. Serve sauce over macaroni. Garnish with thinly sliced cucumber if desired.

4 servings

*1 can (6¾ ounces) skinless boneless pink salmon, drained and flaked, can be substituted for the salmon fillets. Do not cook.

PER SERVING: Calories 225; Protein 17 g; Carbohydrate 29 g; Fat 4 g; Cholesterol 20 mg; Sodium 310 mg

Creamy Fish Chowder

This rich-looking chowder is light on fat but full of flavor.

2 cups cubed potatoes (about 2 medium)
1 cup ¼-inch slices carrots (about 2 medium)
½ cup chopped onion (about 1 medium)
1 cup clam juice
1 cup water
1 tablespoon reduced-calorie margarine
½ teaspoon salt
¼ teaspoon pepper
1 pound haddock or other lean fish fillets, cut into 1-inch pieces
1 can (6½ ounces) whole clams, undrained
1 can (12 ounces) evaporated skim milk
2 tablespoons chopped fresh chives
1 teaspoon paprika

Heat potatoes, carrots, onion, clam juice, water, margarine, salt and pepper to boiling in 3-quart saucepan; reduce heat. Cover and simmer 15 to 20 minutes or until potatoes are almost tender.

Stir in fish and clams. Cover and heat to boiling; reduce heat. Simmer about 5 minutes or until fish flakes easily with fork. Stir in milk, chives and paprika; heat through. **8 servings**

PER SERVING: Calories 225; Protein 19 g; Carbohydrate 32 g; Fat 2 g; Cholesterol 35 mg; Sodium 1070 mg

Scallops with Vegetables

Can't find bay scallops? Use sea scallops and cut them in halves or quarters so they are approximately ½ inch in diameter. This way the same cooking time can be used.

1 pound bay scallops
¼ cup sliced green onions (about 3 medium)
¼ teaspoon salt
⅛ teaspoon white pepper
1 clove garlic, finely chopped
1 package (9 ounces) frozen artichoke hearts, thawed and drained, or 1 can (14 ounces) artichoke hearts, drained and cut into fourths
1 cup cherry tomatoes (about 10), cut into fourths
1 cup shredded romaine or spinach
1 tablespoon lemon juice

Cook scallops, onions, salt, pepper and garlic in 10-inch nonstick skillet over medium-high heat 4 minutes, stirring frequently. Stir in artichoke hearts. Cook 3 to 4 minutes or until scallops are white. Stir in tomatoes and romaine. Cook until tomatoes are hot and romaine is wilted, stirring occasionally; drain. Sprinkle with lemon juice.   **4 servings**

PER SERVING: Calories 160; Protein 28 g; Carbohydrate 12 g; Fat 2 g; Cholesterol 60 mg; Sodium 460 mg

Curried Scallops

3 tablespoons margarine or butter
1 pound sea scallops, cut in half
3 green onions, chopped
1 tablespoon all-purpose flour
1 tablespoon curry powder
½ teaspoon salt
½ cup chicken broth
½ cup milk
1 medium tomato, chopped (about ½ cup)
3 cups hot cooked rice

Heat 1 tablespoon of the margarine in 10-inch skillet over medium-high heat until melted. Cook scallops in margarine 4 to 5 minutes, stirring frequently, until scallops are white. Remove from skillet; drain skillet.

Heat remaining 2 tablespoons margarine in same skillet. Cook onions, flour, curry powder and salt over medium heat, stirring constantly, until bubbly; remove from heat. Stir in chicken broth and milk. Heat to boiling, stirring constantly. Boil and stir 1 minute. Stir in tomato and scallops. Heat about 3 minutes, stirring occasionally. Serve over rice.   **6 servings**

PER SERVING: Calories 230; Protein 12 g; Carbohydrate 30 g; Fat 7 g; Cholesterol 20 mg; Sodium 810 mg

Southwest Scallops

Can't find Anaheim chiles? Use a small red bell pepper. It will also give the sauce a milder and sweeter flavor.

1 red Anaheim chile, chopped
¼ cup sliced green onions (about 3 medium)
2 tablespoons reduced-calorie margarine
2 tablespoons lime juice
2 pounds sea scallops
2 cups cubed fresh pineapple
1 cup Chinese pea pod halves (about 3 ounces)
3 cups hot cooked fettuccine

Cook chile, onions, margarine and lime juice in 10-inch skillet, stirring occasionally, until margarine is melted. Carefully stir in scallops. Cook over medium heat about 12 minutes, stirring frequently, until scallops are white. Stir in pineapple and pea pods. Heat until hot. Remove scallop mixture with slotted spoon; keep warm.

Heat liquid in skillet to boiling. Boil until slightly thickened and reduced to about half. Spoon scallop mixture onto fettuccine; pour liquid over scallop mixture.   **6 servings**

PER SERVING: Calories 335; Protein 39 g; Carbohydrate 34 g; Fat 6 g; Cholesterol 80 mg; Sodium 430 mg

Cajun Seafood and Noodles

If frozen shrimp and crab are not readily available, canned shrimp and crab are just as delicious.

6 ounces uncooked medium noodles (about 3 cups)
1 tablespoon vegetable oil
¾ cup chopped green bell pepper (about 1 medium)
½ cup chopped onion (about 1 medium)
2 tablespoons chopped parsley
⅛ teaspoon ground red pepper (cayenne)
⅛ teaspoon pepper
2 cloves garlic, finely chopped
1 tablespoon all-purpose flour
1 can (16 ounces) whole tomatoes, undrained
1 package (10 ounces) frozen cut okra, thawed
1 package (6 ounces) frozen cooked small shrimp, thawed and drained
1 package (6 ounces) frozen crabmeat, thawed, drained and cartilage removed

Cook noodles as directed on package; drain. Heat oil in 10-inch nonstick skillet over medium heat. Cook bell pepper, onion, parsley, red pepper, pepper and garlic 3 minutes, stirring frequently. Stir in flour and tomatoes; break up tomatoes.

Cook uncovered, stirring frequently, until mixture thickens and boils. Stir in okra, shrimp and crabmeat. Cook uncovered 5 minutes, stirring occasionally. Serve over noodles.   **6 servings**

PER SERVING: Calories 225; Protein 15 g; Carbohydrate 31 g; Fat 5 g; Cholesterol 85 mg; Sodium 240 mg

Cajun Seafood and Noodles

Seafood Pasta with Vegetables

½ cup chopped onion (about 1 medium)
2 cloves garlic, finely chopped
2 teaspoons vegetable oil
2 tablespoons cornstarch
1¾ cups clam- and tomato-flavored
  cocktail
½ pound bay scallops*
1 pound frozen, peeled and deveined,
  medium-size raw shrimp, thawed
2 cups ¼-inch slices yellow squash
  (about 2 small)
1 medium green bell pepper, cut into
  ¼-inch strips
2 tablespoons chopped fresh or 2 teaspoons dried basil leaves
1 teaspoon salt
¼ teaspoon pepper
6 ounces rotini or spiral macaroni,
  cooked and drained
1 cup 1-inch tomato pieces (about 1
  medium)
2 tablespoons chopped parsley

Cook and stir onion and garlic in oil in 4-quart
nonstick Dutch oven over medium heat until
onion is tender. Mix cornstarch and clam- and
tomato-flavored cocktail; stir into onion mixture.
Cook and stir until thickened and bubbly. Stir
scallops, shrimp, squash, bell pepper, basil, salt
and pepper into onion mixture. Cover and cook
until seafood is done and vegetables are crisp-
tender, about 5 minutes. Stir in rotini, tomato
and parsley; heat through.   **8 servings**

*Sea scallops, cut into ½-inch pieces, can be substituted for
bay scallops.

PER SERVING: Calories 360; Protein 16 g; Carbohydrate 54 g; Fat 9 g; Cholesterol 195 mg; Sodium 1760 mg

Noodles with White Clam Sauce

1 medium onion, chopped (about ½ cup)
1 clove garlic, crushed
3 tablespoons margarine
3 tablespoons all-purpose flour
3 cans (6½ ounces each) minced clams,
  undrained
½ teaspoon salt
½ teaspoon dried basil leaves
⅛ teaspoon pepper
¼ cup chopped parsley
4 to 5 cups hot cooked noodles
Grated Parmesan cheese

Cook and stir onion and garlic in margarine in
2-quart saucepan until onion is tender. Stir in
flour. Stir in clams, salt, basil and pepper. Heat
to boiling; reduce heat. Cover and simmer 5
minutes. Stir in parsley. Serve over noodles.
Sprinkle with cheese.   **6 servings**

MICROWAVE DIRECTIONS: Place onion, garlic and
margarine in 2-quart microwavable casserole.
Microwave uncovered on high 2 to 3 minutes or
until onion is tender. Stir in flour. Stir in clams,
salt, basil and pepper. Microwave uncovered 5
to 6 minutes, stirring every 2 minutes, until
slightly thickened and bubbly. Stir in parsley. Let
stand on flat, heatproof surface 5 minutes (not
on wire rack).

PER SERVING: Calories 225; Protein 13 g; Carbohydrate 33 g; Fat 8 g; Cholesterol 35 mg; Sodium 490 mg

Manhattan Clam Chowder

2 slices thin-sliced bacon, finely chopped
¼ cup chopped onion (about 1 small)
1 pint shucked clams with liquor*
2 cups finely chopped potatoes (about 2 medium)
⅓ cup chopped celery
1 cup water
2 teaspoons chopped parsley
1 teaspoon chopped fresh or ¼ teaspoon dried thyme leaves
½ teaspoon salt
⅛ teaspoon pepper
1 can (16 ounces) whole tomatoes, undrained

Cook bacon and onion in 3-quart saucepan, stirring occasionally, until bacon is crisp and onion is softened. Stir in clams, clam liquor, potatoes, celery and water. Heat to boiling; reduce heat. Cover and simmer about 10 minutes or until potatoes are tender. Stir in remaining ingredients; break up tomatoes. Heat to boiling, stirring occasionally. **4 servings**

*2 cans (6½ ounces each) minced clams, undrained, can be substituted for fresh clams. Stir in clams with remaining ingredients.

PER SERVING: Calories 80; Protein 7 g; Carbohydrate 10 g; Fat 2 g; Cholesterol 15 mg; Sodium 540 mg

Chinese Oyster Stew

1 can (10¾ ounces) condensed chicken broth
1 soup can water
2 tablespoons soy sauce
¼ teaspoon grated gingerroot
1 pint shucked large oysters, undrained
2 cups chopped Chinese cabbage
8 ounces sliced mushrooms (about 2½ cups)
½ cup bean sprouts
4 green onions, cut into 1-inch pieces

Heat broth, water, soy sauce and gingerroot to boiling in 3-quart saucepan. Add oysters, cabbage, mushrooms and bean sprouts. Heat to boiling; reduce heat. Cover and simmer about 2 minutes or until cabbage is crisp-tender. Ladle stew into bowls and garnish with green onions. **4 servings**

PER SERVING: Calories 135; Protein 17 g; Carbohydrate 10 g; Fat 3 g; Cholesterol 60 mg; Sodium 1100 mg

Seafood Stew with Rosmarina

½ cup chopped green onions (about 6
  medium)
1 clove garlic, finely chopped
1 teaspoon vegetable oil
1 cup coarsely chopped tomato (about 1
  large)
½ cup thinly sliced carrot (about 1
  medium)
⅓ cup uncooked rosmarina (orzo) pasta
1 can (14½ ounces) chicken broth
1 bottle (8 ounces) clam juice
½ cup dry white wine or chicken broth
1 tablespoon chopped fresh or 1 teaspoon dried thyme leaves
2 teaspoons chopped fresh or ½ teaspoon dried dill weed
¼ teaspoon salt
6 drops red pepper sauce
½ pound red snapper fillets, skinned and
  cut into ½-inch pieces
12 mussels, scrubbed and debearded
8 medium raw shrimp, peeled and
  deveined
½ cup sliced fresh mushrooms
Chopped parsley
Lemon wedges

Cook onions and garlic in oil in nonstick Dutch oven over medium heat about 5 minutes, stirring occasionally. Stir in tomato, carrot, pasta, broth, clam juice, wine, thyme, dill weed, salt and pepper sauce. Heat to boiling; reduce heat. Cover and simmer about 20 minutes, stirring occasionally, until pasta is almost tender.

Stir in red snapper, mussels, shrimp and mushrooms. Cover and heat to boiling; reduce heat. Simmer 6 to 8 minutes, stirring occasionally, until fish flakes easily with fork and mussels open. Sprinkle with parsley. Serve with lemon wedges. **4 servings**

PER SERVING: Calories 430; Protein 21 g; Carbohydrate 57 g; Fat 6 g; Cholesterol 50 mg; Sodium 900 mg

The Cooking Connection

The way you cook can be just as important as what you choose to cook. Consider investing in nonstick cookware and use a nonstick cooking spray. Many cooking methods enable you to use significantly less fat and still prepare a tasty meal. A brief descriiption of some of these cooking methods follows.

- **Grill** or **roast** meat on a rack. This allows the fat to drip off instead of pooling around the meat where it can be reabsorbed.

- **Microwave** foods. Minimal amounts of added fat or liquid are needed, thereby reducing calories from added fat and minimizing loss of water-soluble vitamins in cooking liquids.

- **Pan-broil** foods by starting with a cold, ungreased skillet in which meats are cooked slowly. Fat is poured off as it accumulates, before it can be reabsorbed.

- **Poach** foods by simmering them in a hot liquid just below the boiling point. No added fat is necessary.

- **Steam** foods in a steamer basket over boiling water. This allows foods such as vegetables to retain their water-soluble vitamins.

- **Stir-fry** foods in a small amount of oil. Cook small, uniform pieces of food over high heat, stirring constantly. A wok or large skillet is used to stir-fry.

Shrimp Gumbo

You can substitute 3 cups cut-up chicken for the shrimp if you like.

2 tablespoons reduced-calorie margarine
2 medium onions, sliced
1 medium green bell pepper, cut into thin strips
2 cloves garlic, crushed
2 tablespoons all-purpose flour
3 cups beef broth
½ teaspoon red pepper sauce
¼ teaspoon salt
¼ teaspoon pepper
1 bay leaf
1 package (10 ounces) frozen cut okra, thawed, or 1 can (16 ounces) okra, drained
1 can (16 ounces) whole tomatoes, undrained
1 can (6 ounces) tomato paste
1½ pounds fresh or frozen raw medium shrimp (in shells)*
3 cups hot cooked rice
¼ cup chopped parsley

Heat margarine in Dutch oven over medium heat. Cook onions, bell pepper and garlic, stirring occasionally, until onions are softened. Stir in flour. Cook, stirring constantly, until bubbly; remove from heat. Stir in remaining ingredients except shrimp, rice and parsley; break up tomatoes. Heat to boiling; reduce heat. Simmer uncovered 45 minutes, stirring occasionally.

Peel shrimp. (If shrimp are frozen, do not thaw; peel in cold water.) Make a shallow cut lengthwise down back of each shrimp; wash out vein. Stir shrimp into soup. Cover and simmer about 5 minutes or until shrimp are pink. Remove bay leaf. Serve soup over rice and sprinkle with parsley. **6 servings**

*1 pound frozen peeled and deveined raw shrimp, thawed, can be substituted for the 1½ pounds shrimp in shells.

PER SERVING: Calories 320; Protein 19 g; Carbohydrate 49 g; Fat 6 g; Cholesterol 190 mg; Sodium 950 mg

Spinach Frittata with Creole Sauce (page 51)

3

Satisfying Poultry and Meatless Main Dishes

Chutney Chicken

Chutney is a chunky, sweet-and-sour Indian condiment. The most popular commercial variety is made with mango.

3-pound broiler-fryer chicken, cut up and skinned
¼ cup chopped chutney
¼ cup lime juice
2 tablespoons finely chopped onion
2 tablespoons nonfat plain yogurt
½ teaspoon curry powder
¼ teaspoon dry mustard
1 lime, cut into wedges

Remove excess fat from chicken. Mix all ingredients except chicken and lime wedges in glass or plastic bowl or heavy plastic bag. Add chicken, turning to coat. Cover and refrigerate at least 2 hours.

Heat oven to 375°. Remove chicken from marinade; reserve marinade. Place chicken, meaty sides up, in rectangular pan, 13 × 9 × 2 inches. Pour reserved marinade over chicken. Cover and bake 30 minutes; spoon pan juices over chicken. Bake uncovered until thickest pieces are done, about 30 minutes longer. Arrange on serving platter; pour sauce over chicken. Serve with lime wedges. **6 servings**

MICROWAVE DIRECTIONS: Prepare chicken as directed. Arrange chicken, meaty sides up, thickest parts to outside edges, in rectangular microwavable dish, 12 × 7½ × 2 inches. Pour reserved marinade over chicken. Cover with waxed paper and microwave on high 10 minutes; spoon pan juices over chicken. Rotate dish ½ turn. Cover and microwave until thickest pieces are done, 6 to 10 minutes longer. Serve with lime wedges.

PER SERVING: Calories 145; Protein 23 g; Carbohydrate 7 g; Fat 2 g; Cholesterol 60 mg; Sodium 70 mg

Scandinavian Chicken with Apricots

For a delicious difference, substitute dried apples and apple brandy for the apricots and apricot brandy.

½ cup water
¼ cup apricot brandy
1 package (6 ounces) dried apricots
  (about 1¼ cups)
2 tablespoons currants
1 tablespoon vegetable oil
6 skinless, boneless chicken breast
  halves (about 1½ pounds)
½ teaspoon salt
2 teaspoons chopped fresh or ½ teaspoon dried thyme leaves
¼ teaspoon pepper
1 lemon, thinly sliced
⅓ cup slivered almonds, toasted (if
  desired)

Mix water, brandy, apricots and currants; let stand 15 minutes.

Heat oil in 12-inch nonstick skillet. Cook chicken over medium heat about 15 minutes or until brown on all sides; drain fat. Sprinkle chicken with salt, thyme and pepper. Add apricot mixture and lemon slices. Heat to boiling; reduce heat. Cover and simmer 35 to 40 minutes, spooning pan juices over chicken occasionally, until juices of chicken run clear. Sprinkle with almonds.

6 servings

PER SERVING: Calories 250; Protein 28 g; Carbohydrate 18 g; Fat 4 g; Cholesterol 70 mg; Sodium 260 mg

Lemon Chicken

6 small skinless, boneless chicken breast
  halves (about 3 pounds)
2 tablespoons reduced-calorie margarine
½ cup dry white wine or chicken broth
1 tablespoon lemon juice
¼ teaspoon salt
¼ teaspoon chopped fresh or ⅛ teaspoon dried dill weed
½ lemon, thinly sliced
2 tablespoons sliced green onions

Remove excess fat from chicken. Cook chicken in margarine in 10-inch nonstick skillet over medium heat, turning once, until light brown, about 10 minutes. Mix wine, lemon juice, salt and dill weed; pour over chicken. Place lemon slices on chicken. Heat to boiling; reduce heat. Cover and simmer until chicken is done, 10 to 15 minutes. Remove chicken; keep warm. Heat wine mixture to boiling; cook until reduced by half, about 3 minutes. Pour over chicken; sprinkle with onions.

6 servings

MICROWAVE DIRECTIONS: Decrease wine to ¼ cup. Place margarine in 3-quart microwavable casserole. Microwave uncovered on high until melted, about 1½ minutes. Arrange chicken in margarine, thickest parts to outside edges. Cover tightly and microwave 4 minutes. Mix wine, lemon juice, salt and dill weed; pour over chicken. Place lemon slices on chicken; rotate casserole ½ turn. Cover tightly and microwave until chicken is done, 4 to 6 minutes longer. Let stand covered 5 minutes; sprinkle with onions.

PER SERVING: Calories 230; Protein 33 g; Carbohydrate 1 g; Fat 6 g; Cholesterol 85 mg; Sodium 200 mg

Chicken Breasts Dijon

For an easy change of pace, try different types of mustard in this dish.

6 small skinless, boneless chicken breast
   halves (about 3 pounds)
¼ cup Dijon mustard
1 teaspoon vegetable oil
2 tablespoons dry white wine or chicken
   broth
Coarsely ground pepper
2 tablespoons mustard seed

Heat oven to 400°. Remove excess fat from chicken. Place chicken, meaty sides up, in rectangular pan, 13 × 9 × 2 inches, sprayed with nonstick cooking spray. Mix mustard, oil and wine; brush over chicken. Sprinkle with pepper and mustard seed. Bake uncovered until chicken is done, about 30 minutes. Sprinkle with chopped parsley if desired.   **6 servings**

PER SERVING: Calories 270; Protein 46 g; Carbohydrate 2 g; Fat 7 g; Cholesterol 120 mg; Sodium 230 mg

Oriental Barbecued Chicken

If you like, you can substitute 1 pound boneless, skinless chicken thighs for the chicken breast halves.

4 skinless, boneless chicken breast
   halves (about 1 pound)
½ cup Hoisin sauce
1 tablespoon sesame oil
1 tablespoon tomato paste
½ teaspoon ground ginger
2 cloves garlic, crushed

Set oven control to broil. Trim fat from chicken breast halves; place on rack in broiler pan. Mix remaining ingredients; brush on chicken.

Broil with tops about 4 inches from heat 7 to 8 minutes or until brown; turn. Brush with sauce. Broil 4 to 5 minutes longer or until chicken is done. Heat remaining sauce to boiling. Serve with chicken.   **4 servings**

PER SERVING: Calories 175; Protein 27 g; Carbohydrate 2 g; Fat 5 g; Cholesterol 70 mg; Sodium 150 mg

---

If you like casseroles, try eliminating hidden calories by making the following substitutions:

FOR:	SUBSTITUTE:	FOR:	SUBSTITUTE:
Margarine or butter (1 tablespoon = 100 calories)	Reduced-calorie margarine (1 tablespoon = 50 calories)	Cheddar cheese (1 cup shredded [4 ounces] = 460 calories)	Low-fat Cheddar cheese (1 cup shredded [4 ounces] = 200 calories)
Tuna canned in oil (6 ounces = 340 calories)	Tuna canned in water (6 ounces = 220 calories)	Whole Milk (1 cup = 160 calories)	Skim milk (1 cup = 90 calories)
Almonds or peanuts (½ cup = 430 calories)	Waterchestnuts (½ cup sliced = 70 calories)		

Chicken Breasts with Sun-dried–Tomato Sauce

Chicken Breasts with Sun-dried–Tomato Sauce

Use plain sun-dried tomatoes rather than those packed in oil.

¼ cup coarsely chopped sun-dried
    tomatoes
½ cup chicken broth
4 skinless, boneless chicken breast
    halves (about 1 pound)
½ cup sliced fresh mushrooms
2 tablespoons chopped green onions
2 cloves garlic, finely chopped
2 tablespoons dry red wine or chicken
    broth
1 teaspoon vegetable oil
½ cup skim milk
2 teaspoons cornstarch
2 teaspoons chopped fresh or ½ tea-
    spoon dried basil leaves
2 cups hot cooked fettuccine or rice

Mix tomatoes and broth; let stand 30 minutes.

Trim fat from chicken. Cook mushrooms, onions and garlic in wine in 10-inch nonstick skillet over medium heat about 3 minutes, stirring occasionally, until mushrooms are tender; remove mixture from skillet. Add oil to skillet. Cook chicken in oil over medium heat until brown on both sides. Add tomato mixture. Heat to boiling; reduce heat. Cover and simmer about 10 minutes, stirring occasionally, until chicken is done. Remove chicken; keep warm. Mix milk, cornstarch and basil; stir into tomato mixture. Heat to boiling, stirring constantly. Boil and stir 1 minute. Stir in mushroom mixture; heat through. Serve over chicken and fettuccine. **4 servings**

MICROWAVE DIRECTIONS: Decrease broth to ¼ cup. Omit oil. Decrease milk to ¼ cup. Mix tomatoes and broth as directed. Trim fat from chicken. Place mushrooms, onions, garlic and wine in 4-cup microwavable measure. Cover tightly and microwave on high 2 to 3 minutes or until mushrooms are tender; reserve. Place chicken in 2-quart microwavable casserole. Pour tomato mixture over chicken. Cover tightly and microwave on high 10 to 12 minutes, rotating casserole ¼ turn every 3 minutes, until chicken is done. Remove chicken; keep warm. Mix milk, cornstarch and basil; stir into tomato mixture. Microwave uncovered 2 to 4 minutes, stirring every minute, until mixture thickens and boils. Stir in mushroom mixture. Microwave uncovered 30 to 60 seconds or until mixture boils. Serve over chicken and fettuccine.

PER SERVING: Calories 345; Protein 46 g; Carbohydrate 28 g; Fat 4 g; Cholesterol 100 mg; Sodium 240 mg

Chicken en Papillote

2 whole chicken breasts (about 1½ pounds)
6 cups chopped fresh spinach
¼ cup shredded provolone cheese (1 ounce)
1 tablespoon chopped sun-dried tomatoes
1 clove garlic, finely chopped
½ lemon
Paprika, if desired
4 twelve-inch-square pieces cooking parchment paper or aluminum foil

Remove skin and bones from chicken breasts. Cut chicken breasts in half. Flatten each half to ¼-inch thickness between plastic wrap or waxed paper. Cover and cook spinach in 2-quart saucepan over medium heat 2 to 3 minutes or until wilted; drain thoroughly. Reserve 2 tablespoons spinach.

Heat oven to 400°. Mix reserved spinach, the cheese, tomatoes and garlic. Spoon one-fourth of the spinach mixture on one side of each chicken breast half. Fold chicken over filling. Squeeze lemon over chicken. Sprinkle with paprika.

Cut each piece of parchment paper into a 12-inch circle. Spoon one-fourth of the cooked spinach onto half of each circle. Place one stuffed chicken breast half on spinach. Fold other half of paper circle over chicken. Seal edges by turning up and folding together. Twist ends several times to secure packet. Bake on cookie sheet about 15 minutes or until paper puffs up and is light brown. To serve, cut a large X shape on top of each packet and fold back corners.   **4 servings**

MICROWAVE DIRECTIONS: Do not use aluminum foil. Arrange sealed packets in circle in microwave oven. Microwave on high 8 to 10 minutes, rearranging packets after 4 minutes, until paper puffs up. Continue as directed.

PER SERVING: Calories 180; Protein 28 g; Carbohydrate 3 g; Fat 6 g; Cholesterol 85 mg; Sodium 215 mg

Chicken-Basil Noodles

2 teaspoons olive or vegetable oil
½ cup finely chopped onion (about 1 medium)
1 clove garlic, finely chopped
2½ cups chopped tomatoes (about 3 medium)
2 cups cubed cooked chicken or turkey
¼ cup chopped fresh or 1 tablespoon dried basil leaves
½ teaspoon salt
⅛ teaspoon red pepper sauce
4 ounces uncooked noodles (about 2 cups)

Heat oil in 10-inch nonstick skillet over medium-high heat. Cook onion and garlic in oil until softened. Stir in remaining ingredients except noodles; reduce heat to medium. Cover and cook about 5 minutes, stirring frequently, until mixture is hot and tomatoes are soft. Cook noodles as directed on package; drain. Serve chicken mixture over noodles.   **4 servings**

PER SERVING: Calories 280; Protein 24 g; Carbohydrate 28 g; Fat 8 g; Cholesterol 60 mg; Sodium 330 mg

Orange Stir-fried Chicken

Nonstick cookware is invaluable for low-fat cooking. It allows you to cook with less fat, and food won't stick to the pan.

    4 skinless, boneless chicken breast
      halves (about 1 pound)
    1 tablespoon low-sodium soy sauce
    1 teaspoon cornstarch
    1 teaspoon grated gingerroot or ½ tea-
      spoon ground ginger
    1 clove garlic, finely chopped
    ½ cup orange juice
    2 teaspoons cornstarch
    2 teaspoons vegetable oil
    3 cups thinly sliced fresh mushrooms
      (about 8 ounces)
    ½ cup coarsely shredded carrot (about 1
      medium)
    2 cups hot cooked rice

Trim fat from chicken breast halves. Cut chicken into ¼-inch strips. Mix soy sauce, 1 teaspoon cornstarch, the gingerroot and garlic in medium glass or plastic bowl. Stir in chicken. Cover and refrigerate 30 minutes.

Mix orange juice and 2 teaspoons cornstarch until cornstarch is dissolved. Heat 1 teaspoon of the oil in 10-inch nonstick skillet over high heat. Add chicken mixture; stir-fry until chicken turns white. Remove chicken from skillet.

Add remaining 1 teaspoon oil to skillet. Add mushrooms and carrot; stir-fry about 3 minutes or until mushrooms are tender. Stir in chicken and orange juice mixture. Heat to boiling, stirring constantly. Boil and stir about 30 seconds or until thickened. Serve over rice.

4 servings

PER SERVING: Calories 335; Protein 31 g; Carbohydrate 40 g; Fat 5 g; Cholesterol 70 mg; Sodium 240 mg

Healthful Staples to Keep on Hand

Keep a plentiful supply of healthy staples in the house to be certain that you have what you need when preparing meals. The list that follows contains items you will use frequently and that you can stock up on easily.

Herbs and Spices Dried or fresh (chopped and frozen), these are essentials for any healthy cooking. Herbs and spices enhance foods and boost flavor without adding extra fat or salt. Stock your cabinets with basil, bay leaves, dill weed, oregano, garlic, ginger, red pepper sauce, ground red pepper, salt, chile powder, curry powder, pepper, cinnamon, nutmeg and cloves. Items such as garlic and oregano can be purchased prechopped or minced but must be refrigerated after opening.

Baking and Cooking Essentials Cornstarch, baking powder, baking soda, flour, rolled oats, raisins, vegetable oil(s), vinegar(s) and reduced-sodium soy sauce should be mainstays in any kitchen.

Whole Grains, Dried Beans and Pasta These items can be kept as staples because they remain edible indefinitely. For optimum flavor, store tightly sealed in a cool, dry place and use within one year of purchase.

Perishables Foods that will not last for long periods of time, but that you will probably use quite frequently include nonfat or low-fat yogurt, other dairy products, lemons, carrots, celery, onions and potatoes.

Curried Chicken and Nectarines

Curried Chicken and Nectarines

4 skinless, boneless chicken breast
  halves (about 1 pound)
2 tablespoons reduced-calorie oil-and-vin-
  egar dressing
1 teaspoon curry powder
¼ cup raisins
¼ cup sliced green onions
¼ teaspoon salt
1 medium bell pepper, cut into ¼-inch
  strips
2 small nectarines, cut into ¼-inch slices

Trim fat from chicken breast halves. Cut chicken crosswise into ½-inch strips. Mix dressing and curry powder in medium bowl. Add chicken; toss. Heat 10-inch nonstick skillet over medium-high heat. Stir in chicken and remaining ingredients except nectarines; stir-fry 4 to 6 minutes or until chicken is done. Stir in nectarines carefully; heat through. Serve with hot cooked rice or couscous if desired.   **4 servings**

MICROWAVE DIRECTIONS: Prepare chicken as directed. Mix dressing and curry powder in 2-quart microwavable casserole. Add chicken; toss. Stir in remaining ingredients except nectarines. Cover tightly and microwave on high 8 to 10 minutes, stirring after 4 minutes, until chicken is done. Stir in nectarines carefully. Cover and microwave 1 minute or until heated through.

PER SERVING: Calories 210; Protein 25 g; Carbohydrate 15 g; Fat 6 g; Cholesterol 80 mg; Sodium 230 mg

Caribbean Chicken

The Caribbean flair in this dish comes from black beans, lime, gingerroot and mango. Try substituting papaya for the mango.

4 chicken drumsticks (about 1 pound)
4 chicken thighs (about 1 pound)
1 cup cubed mango or 1 can (8 ounces)
  peach slices, drained and cut up
1 tablespoon grated gingerroot or 1 teaspoon ground ginger
2 tablespoons lime juice
1 teaspoon finely shredded lime peel
½ teaspoon salt
1 clove garlic, finely chopped
2 green onions, thinly sliced
2 cans (15 ounces each) black beans,
  undrained

Heat oven to 375°. Place chicken pieces, skin sides up, in ungreased rectangular baking dish, 13 × 9 × 2 inches. Bake uncovered 40 minutes. Remove excess fat. Mix remaining ingredients. Spoon over and around chicken. Cover and bake 30 minutes longer or until juices of chicken run clear.   **4 servings**

MICROWAVE DIRECTIONS: Arrange chicken pieces, skin sides up and thickest parts to outside edges, in rectangular microwavable dish, 12 × 7½ × 2 inches. Cover tightly and microwave on high 9 minutes. Remove excess fat. Rotate dish ½ turn. Mix remaining ingredients. Spoon over and around chicken pieces. Cover tightly and microwave on high about 8 minutes longer or until juices of chicken run clear. Let stand 3 minutes.

PER SERVING: Calories 310; Protein 32 g; Carbohydrate 26 g; Fat 9 g; Cholesterol 90 mg; Sodium 760 mg

Southwest Chicken Soup

Southwest Chicken Soup

You can substitute marinated or pickled red peppers for the fresh. They are available in many supermarkets in the refrigerated or shelf-stable sections. Be sure to drain the light brine in which they are packaged before using.

**2 large red bell peppers
4 boneless, skinless chicken breast halves (about 1 pound)
½ cup chopped onion (about 1 medium)
3 cups chicken broth
2 tablespoons lime juice
1 tablespoon chopped cilantro
½ teaspoon salt
¼ teaspoon pepper
2 cloves garlic, crushed
2 cups cubed jicama**

Set oven control to broil. Place bell peppers on rack in broiler pan. Broil with tops about 5 inches from heat, turning occasionally, until skin is blistered and evenly browned (not burned). Remove peppers to brown paper bag and close tightly. Let stand 20 minutes.

Place chicken breast halves on rack in broiler pan. Broil with tops 5 to 7 inches from heat about 15 minutes, turning once, until juices of chicken run clear. Cool 10 minutes. Cut into bite-size pieces.

Peel peppers; discard skin. Place peppers and onion in blender or food processor. Cover and blend, or process, until smooth.

Heat pepper mixture, broth, lime juice, cilantro, salt, pepper and garlic to boiling in 2-quart saucepan; reduce heat. Simmer uncovered 15 minutes, stirring occasionally. Stir in chicken and jicama. Heat until hot.   **4 servings**

PER SERVING: Calories 215; Protein 33 g; Carbohydrate 13 g; Fat 3 g; Cholesterol 70 mg; Sodium 980 mg

Spinach Frittata with Creole Sauce

**Creole Sauce (below)
¼ cup chopped onion (about 1 small)
2 teaspoons margarine
3 cups coarsely chopped spinach (about 4 ounces)
1½ cups cholesterol-free egg product
½ teaspoon chopped fresh or ⅛ teaspoon dried thyme leaves
⅛ teaspoon salt
⅛ teaspoon pepper
2 tablespoons shredded part-skim mozzarella cheese**

Prepare Creole Sauce; keep warm. Cook onion in margarine in 10-inch nonstick skillet over medium heat about 3 minutes, stirring occasionally. Add spinach; toss just until spinach is wilted.

Beat egg product, thyme, salt and pepper; pour over spinach. Cover and cook over medium-low heat 5 to 7 minutes or until eggs are set and light brown on bottom. Sprinkle with cheese. Cut into wedges. Serve with Creole Sauce.
4 servings

Creole Sauce

**1 cup coarsely chopped tomato (about 1 large)
¼ cup chopped onion (about 1 small)
2 tablespoons sliced celery
¼ teaspoon paprika
⅛ teaspoon pepper
4 drops red pepper sauce**

Heat all ingredients to boiling in 1-quart saucepan, stirring occasionally; reduce heat. Simmer uncovered about 5 minutes, stirring occasionally, until thickened.

PER SERVING: Calories 95; Protein 11 g; Carbohydrate 7 g; Fat 3 g; Cholesterol 5 mg; Sodium 275 mg

Mexican Strata

Mexican Strata

Whole-grain bread gives this do-ahead dish a nice hearty texture, but white bread can be used too.

8 slices whole-grain bread (crusts removed)
1½ cups shredded low-fat Cheddar cheese (6 ounces)
1 can (4 ounces) chopped green chiles, well drained
1 jar (2 ounces) sliced pimientos, well drained
1⅓ cups skim milk
¼ teaspoon ground cumin
6 egg whites or 1 cup cholesterol-free egg product

Spray square baking dish, 8 × 8 × 2 inches, with nonstick cooking spray. Place 4 slices bread in dish. Sprinkle with cheese, chiles and pimientos. Top with remaining bread. Beat remaining ingredients; pour over bread. Cover and refrigerate at least 2 hours but no longer than 24 hours.

Heat oven to 325°. Bake 1 hour to 1 hour 15 minutes or until set and top is golden brown. Let stand 10 minutes before serving.

4 servings

PER SERVING: Calories 320; Protein 25 g; Carbohydrate 32 g; Fat 9 g; Cholesterol 5 mg; Sodium 830 mg

Three-Cheese Noodle Bake

4 ounces uncooked noodles (about 2 cups)
1 cup low-fat cottage cheese
¾ cup shredded low-fat Cheddar cheese (3 ounces)
½ cup low-fat sour cream
⅓ cup chopped green onions
3 tablespoons grated Parmesan cheese
½ teaspoon Worcestershire sauce
⅛ teaspoon pepper
2 egg whites
1 egg

Heat oven to 350°. Spray square baking dish, 8 × 8 × 2 inches, with nonstick cooking spray. Cook noodles as directed on package; drain. Mix noodles and remaining ingredients. Spread in dish. Bake uncovered 30 to 35 minutes or until center is set and edges are golden brown. Let stand 5 minutes. **4 servings**

PER SERVING: Calories 275; Protein 22 g; Carbohydrate 25 g; Fat 9 g; Cholesterol 80 mg; Sodium 690 mg

Triple-Cheese Ravioli

1 package (8 ounces) dried cheese-filled ravioli or tortellini
2 cups chopped tomatoes (about 2 large or 1 pound)
½ cup sliced mushrooms
¼ cup chopped onion (about 1 small)
¼ cup dry red wine or chicken broth
1 tablespoon chopped fresh or 1 teaspoon dried basil leaves
⅛ teaspoon salt
⅛ teaspoon pepper
1 clove garlic, finely chopped
½ cup low-fat ricotta cheese
2 tablespoons grated Parmesan cheese

Cook ravioli as directed on package; drain. Cook remaining ingredients except cheeses in 10-inch skillet over medium-high heat about 5 minutes, stirring frequently, until tomatoes are soft.

Heat oven to 325°. Place ravioli in ungreased square baking dish, 8 × 8 × 2 inches. Spread ricotta cheese over ravioli. Pour tomato sauce over top. Sprinkle with Parmesan cheese. Bake uncovered about 20 minutes or until hot.

4 servings

PER SERVING: Calories 170; Protein 8 g; Carbohydrate 23 g; Fat 4 g; Cholesterol 30 mg; Sodium 260 mg

Easy Macaroni and Cheese

Our special cheese sauce makes this hearty favorite low in fat.

1 package (7 ounces) macaroni shells
Cheese sauce (below)
2 tablespoons sliced green onions
2 tablespoons chopped red bell pepper

Cook macaroni as directed on package; drain. Prepare Cheese Sauce in 3-quart saucepan. Stir macaroni, onions and bell pepper into sauce. Cook, stirring constantly, until heated through.

4 servings

Cheese Sauce

1 tablespoon margarine
2 tablespoons all-purpose flour
¼ teaspoon salt
¼ teaspoon dry mustard
⅛ teaspoon pepper
1 cup skim milk
1 cup shredded low-fat Cheddar cheese (4 ounces)

Heat margarine in 1½-quart nonstick saucepan over low heat. Stir in flour, salt, mustard and pepper. Cook over low heat, stirring constantly, until margarine is absorbed; remove from heat. Gradually stir in milk. Heat to boiling, stirring constantly. Boil and stir 1 minute. Stir in cheese until melted.

PER SERVING: Calories 245; Protein 11 g; Carbohydrate 35 g; Fat 6 g; Cholesterol 1 mg; Sodium 170 mg

Bean-stuffed Cabbage Rolls

For variety, try different types of beans, such as pinto, kidney or black beans.

1 large head cabbage (about 3 pounds)
1 tablespoon reduced-calorie margarine
¼ cup chopped onion (about 1 small)
2 teaspoons chopped fresh or ½ teaspoon dried sage leaves
¼ teaspoon ground cumin
1 clove garlic, finely chopped
1½ cups finely shredded cabbage
½ cup shredded carrot (about 1 medium)
1 can (19 ounces) cannellini beans, drained
½ cup chicken broth
½ cup skim milk
2 teaspoons cornstarch
1 teaspoon chopped fresh or ¼ teaspoon dried sage leaves
¼ teaspoon salt
6 tablespoons shredded low-fat Swiss cheese

Remove core from cabbage. Cover cabbage with warm water; let stand about 10 minutes or until leaves loosen slightly. Remove 12 cabbage leaves. Cover leaves with boiling water. Cover and let stand about 10 minutes or until leaves are limp; drain.

Heat oven to 350°. Heat margarine in 2-quart nonstick saucepan over medium heat. Cook onion, 2 teaspoons chopped fresh sage, the cumin and garlic about 3 minutes, stirring frequently, until onion is softened. Stir in shredded cabbage, carrot and beans.

Place scant ¼ cup bean mixture at stem end of cabbage leaf. Roll leaf around bean mixture, tucking in sides. Place cabbage rolls, seam sides down, in ungreased rectangular baking dish, 13 × 9 × 2 inches. Pour broth over rolls. Cover and bake 30 to 35 minutes or until rolls are hot.

Remove cabbage rolls with slotted spoon; keep warm. Drain liquid from baking dish, reserving ½ cup. Gradually stir milk into cornstarch in saucepan until smooth; stir in reserved liquid, 1 teaspoon chopped fresh sage and the salt. Heat to boiling over medium heat, stirring constantly. Boil and stir 1 minute. Serve sauce over cabbage rolls; sprinkle each serving with 1 tablespoon cheese. **6 servings**

PER SERVING: Calories 175; Protein 8 g; Carbohydrate 32 g; Fat 3 g; Cholesterol 0 mg; Sodium 440 mg

Vegetables and Hominy

1 package (10 ounces) frozen lima beans
½ cup water
1 cup chopped onion (about 1 large)
3 cups chopped tomatoes (about 3 large)
1 can (14½ ounces) hominy, drained
1 tablespoon chopped fresh or 1 tea-
    spoon dried basil leaves
1 tablespoon chile powder
½ teaspoon salt
⅛ teaspoon pepper
3 medium zucchini, cut lengthwise in
    half, then crosswise into ¼-inch slices

Cook lima beans as directed on package—
except use Dutch oven and add ½ cup additional water and the onion; drain. Stir in
remaining ingredients. Cook uncovered over
medium heat 5 to 10 minutes, stirring occasionally, until zucchini is crisp-tender.

4 servings

PER SERVING; Calories 180; Protein 9 g; Carbohydrate 36 g; Fat 1 g; Cholesterol 0 mg; Sodium 390 mg

Lentil Vegetable Soup

1 cup chopped onion (about 1 large)
2 teaspoons chile powder
1 teaspoon salt
1 teaspoon ground cumin
2 cloves garlic, finely chopped
1 can (6 ounces) spicy tomato juice
3 cups water
1 cup dried lentils (about 6 ounces)
1 can (14½ ounces) whole tomatoes,
    undrained
1 can (4 ounces) chopped green chiles,
    undrained
1 cup fresh or frozen whole kernel corn
2 cups julienne strips zucchini (about 2
    small)

Heat onion, chile powder, salt, cumin, garlic and
tomato juice to boiling in 3-quart saucepan; reduce heat. Cover and simmer 5 minutes. Stir in
remaining ingredients except corn and zucchini.
Heat to boiling; reduce heat. Cover and simmer
20 minutes. Stir in corn; cover and simmer 10
minutes. Stir in zucchini; cover and simmer
about 5 minutes or until lentils and zucchini are
tender. **6 servings**

PER SERVING: Calories 165; Protein 11 g; Carbohydrate 32 g; Fat 1 g; Cholesterol 0 mg; Sodium 590 mg

Lentil Vegetable Soup

Healthy Eating Out of the House and on the Road

We all enjoy, and probably need, a break from preparing meals. With virtually 30 percent of calories and 40 percent of every food dollar spent on foods eaten away from home, knowing how to make healthy choices when eating out is vital.

Low-Fat Tips

- Call in advance to find out if healthy menu items are available. Low-fat choices are often noted on the menu.

- Just as at home, choose lean meats, fish and poultry without skin, and ask that they be prepared with a minimum of added fat. Most chefs are more than willing to broil, grill, bake, steam and poach foods at your request.

- Vegetables are naturally low in fat, but the way they're prepared can quickly change their calorie content. Request plain vegetables; you can add butter or margarine at the table, if you wish. Choose baked potatoes instead of French fried potatoes or chips.

- Salad dressings and sauces may be requested "on the side," so you can decide how much you'd like to use. Just remember that the small dishes in which side items are served often hold much more than the amount a chef would normally add to the food. Beware: In examining plates after a meal, chefs report many diners end up eating *more* of the dressing or sauce than they would have if it had been served on the food.

Hearty Bean and Pasta Stew

1 cup coarsely chopped tomato (about 1 large)
¾ cup uncooked shell macaroni
¼ cup chopped onion (about 1 small)
¼ cup chopped green bell pepper (about ½ small)
1 tablespoon chopped fresh or 1 teaspoon dried basil leaves
1 teaspoon Worcestershire sauce
1 clove garlic, finely chopped
1 can (16 ounces) kidney beans, drained
1 can (8 ounces) garbanzo beans, drained
1 can (14½ ounces) chicken broth

Mix all ingredients in 2-quart saucepan. Heat to boiling, stirring occasionally; reduce heat. Cover and simmer about 15 minutes, stirring occasionally, until macaroni is tender.   **4 servings**

PER SERVING: Calories 350; Protein 20 g; Carbohydrate 59 g; Fat 4 g; Cholesterol 0 mg; Sodium 690 mg

Spicy Vegetable Stew

¾ cup chopped onion
1 clove garlic, finely chopped
2 tablespoons vegetable oil
1 large red bell pepper, cut into
　2 × ½-inch strips
2 medium poblano or Anaheim chiles,
　seeded and cut into 2 × ½-inch strips
1 jalapeño chile, seeded and chopped
1 cup cubed Hubbard or acorn squash
　(about ½ pound)
2 cans (14½ ounces each) chicken broth
½ teaspoon salt
½ teaspoon pepper
½ teaspoon ground coriander
1 cup thinly sliced zucchini (about 1
　small)
1 cup thinly sliced yellow squash (about
　1 small)
1 can (17 ounces) whole kernel corn,
　drained
1 can (16 ounces) pinto beans, drained

Cook onion and garlic in oil in Dutch oven over medium heat, stirring occasionally, until onion is softened. Stir in bell pepper, poblano and jalapeño chiles. Cook 15 minutes, stirring occasionally.

Stir in Hubbard squash, broth, salt, pepper and coriander. Heat to boiling; reduce heat. Cover and simmer about 15 minutes or until squash is tender. Stir in remaining ingredients. Cook uncovered about 10 minutes, stirring occasionally, until zucchini is tender. **6 servings**

PER SERVING: Calories 210; Protein 9 g; Carbohydrate 32 g; Fat 7 g; Cholesterol 0 mg; Sodium 890 mg

Lamb Patties with Fresh Mint Sauce (page 75)

4

Meat Main Dishes

Gingered Flank Steak

Broiling is a great way to keep fat low when cooking meat.

1½-pound lean beef flank steak
⅓ cup lemon juice
2 tablespoons honey
1 tablespoon low-sodium soy sauce
2 teaspoons grated gingerroot or 1 teaspoon ground ginger
2 cloves garlic, crushed

Trim fat from beef steak. Cut both sides of beef into diamond pattern ⅛ inch deep. Place in shallow glass or plastic dish. Mix remaining ingredients; pour over beef. Cover and refrigerate at least 8 hours, turning occasionally.

Set oven control to broil. Spray broiler pan rack with nonstick cooking spray. Remove beef from marinade; reserve marinade. Place beef on rack in broiler pan. Broil with top 3 inches from heat 12 to 14 minutes, turning once and brushing frequently with marinade, until desired doneness. Cut diagonally into thin slices.   **6 servings**

PER SERVING: Calories 215; Protein 30 g; Carbohydrate 7 g; Fat 7 g; Cholesterol 90 mg; Sodium 160 mg

Dilled Steak with Vegetables

1½-pound lean beef bone-in round or
   chuck steak, about ½ inch thick
2 tablespoons all-purpose flour
½ teaspoon salt
⅛ teaspoon pepper
1 tablespoon vegetable oil
½ cup water
2 teaspoons vinegar
½ teaspoon dried dill weed
12 small new potatoes (about 1½
   pounds)
3 medium zucchini, cut into 1-inch slices
¼ cup cold water
2 tablespoons all-purpose flour
½ cup nonfat plain yogurt

Trim fat from beef steak. Mix 2 tablespoons flour, the salt and pepper. Sprinkle 1 side of beef with half of the flour mixture; pound in. Turn beef and pound in remaining flour mixture. Cut beef into 6 serving pieces. Heat oil in 4-quart nonstick Dutch oven. Cook beef in oil over medium heat until brown, about 15 minutes. Mix ½ cup water, the vinegar and dill weed; pour over beef. Heat to boiling; reduce heat. Cover and simmer until beef is just tender, about 45 minutes. Add potatoes; cover and simmer 15 minutes. Add zucchini; cover and simmer until vegetables are tender, 10 to 15 minutes. Remove beef and vegetables; keep warm.

Add enough water to cooking liquid to measure 1 cup. Shake ¼ cup water and 2 tablespoons flour in tightly covered container; gradually stir into cooking liquid. Heat to boiling, stirring constantly. Boil and stir 1 minute. Stir in yogurt; heat just until hot. Serve with beef and vegetables.   **6 servings**

PER SERVING: Calories 240; Protein 23 g; Carbohydrate 24 g; Fat 6 g; Cholesterol 50 mg; Sodium 250 mg

Beef Stroganoff

Our version of this classic lowers fat dramatically but keeps flavor high.

1-pound lean beef boneless round steak,
   about ½ inch thick
1 tablespoon reduced-calorie margarine
½ cup chopped onion (about 1 medium)
1 clove garlic, finely chopped
3 cups sliced mushrooms (about 8
   ounces)
¼ cup dry red wine or beef broth
2 tablespoons cornstarch
1 cup beef broth
¼ teaspoon pepper
¾ cup nonfat plain yogurt
2 cups hot cooked noodles or rice
2 tablespoons chopped parsley

Trim fat from beef steak; cut beef with grain into 2-inch strips. Cut strips diagonally across grain into ¼-inch slices. (For ease in cutting, partially freeze beef, about 1 hour 30 minutes.) Heat margarine in 10-inch nonstick skillet until melted. Add onion and garlic; cook and stir over medium-high heat until onion is tender. Stir in beef and mushrooms; cook and stir until beef is no longer pink. Stir in wine; reduce heat. Cover and simmer 10 minutes.

Stir cornstarch into beef broth until dissolved; stir into beef mixture. Cook and stir over medium-high heat until thickened; remove from heat. Stir in pepper and yogurt; reduce heat. Cover and simmer, stirring occasionally, until beef is tender, about 30 minutes. Serve over noodles; sprinkle with parsley.   **6 servings**

PER SERVING: Calories 230; Protein 22 g; Carbohydrate 21 g; Fat 6 g; Cholesterol 65 mg; Sodium 330 mg

Oriental Beef with Rice Noodles

¾-pound lean beef boneless round steak
2 tablespoons sake (rice wine), sherry or chicken broth
1 tablespoon finely chopped gingerroot or 1 teaspoon ground ginger
2 teaspoons vegetable oil
½ teaspoon salt
1 clove garlic, crushed
4 ounces rice sticks
1 teaspoon vegetable oil
2 cups thinly sliced bok choy with leaves (about 3 large stalks)
½ cup sliced green onions (about 4 medium)
1 can (15 ounces) straw mushrooms, drained*
2 tablespoons sake (rice wine), sherry or chicken broth

Trim fat from beef steak. Cut beef diagonally into ¼-inch strips. (For ease in cutting, partially freeze beef, about 1 hour 30 minutes.) Mix beef, 2 tablespoons sake, the gingerroot, 2 teaspoons oil, the salt and garlic in medium glass or plastic bowl. Cover and refrigerate 30 minutes.

Place rice sticks in large bowl. Cover with hot water. Let stand 10 minutes; drain well. Chop coarsely.

Heat 1 teaspoon oil in wok or 12-inch skillet until very hot. Add beef mixture; stir-fry about 5 minutes or until beef is done. Add rice sticks, bok choy, onions and mushrooms; stir-fry about 4 minutes or until bok choy is crisp-tender. Sprinkle with 2 tablespoons sake. **4 servings**

*2 jars (4.5 ounces each) whole mushrooms, drained, can be substituted for the straw mushrooms.

PER SERVING: Calories 205; Protein 18 g; Carbohydrate 18 g; Fat 5 g; Cholesterol 40 mg; Sodium 380 mg

Beef in Mushroom Sauce

This is a rich-tasting, lower-fat variation on the theme of beef stroganoff.

¾-pound lean beef boneless round steak, about ½ inch thick
2½ cups sliced fresh mushrooms (about 8 ounces)
½ cup chopped onion (about 1 medium)
1 clove garlic, finely chopped
¼ cup dry red wine or beef broth
2 tablespoons cornstarch
1 can (10½ ounces) beef broth
⅛ teaspoon pepper
¾ cup plain nonfat yogurt
2 cups hot cooked rice or cholesterol-free noodles
2 tablespoons chopped parsley

Trim fat from beef steak. Cut beef with grain into 2-inch strips. Cut strips diagonally across grain into ¼-inch slices. (For ease in cutting, partially freeze beef, about 1 hour 15 minutes.)

Spray 10-inch nonstick skillet with nonstick cooking spray. Heat over medium-high heat. Stir beef, mushrooms, onion and garlic into skillet. Cook uncovered about 4 minutes, stirring frequently, until beef is no longer pink. Stir in wine. Heat to boiling; reduce heat. Cover and simmer 10 minutes. Stir cornstarch into broth until dissolved. Stir into beef mixture. Cook over medium-high heat, stirring frequently, until thickened, about 2 minutes; remove from heat. Stir in pepper and yogurt. Heat to boiling; reduce heat. Cover and simmer 30 minutes, stirring occasionally, until beef is tender. Serve over rice. Sprinkle with parsley. **4 servings**

PER SERVING: Calories 370; Protein 32 g; Carbohydrate 43 g; Fat 6 g; Cholesterol 43 mg; Sodium 1040 mg

Moroccan Beef with Couscous

This dish was inspired by the Moroccan recipe for Tangia, named after a type of cooking vessel, the tangia.

1½-pounds beef boneless chuck, tip or round roast, or boneless lamb shoulder cut into 1-inch cubes
1 cup beef broth or water
⅓ cup chopped fresh or 2 tablespoons dried coriander leaves
⅓ cup chopped fresh Italian or regular parsley
1 tablespoon olive or vegetable oil
1 teaspoon ground ginger
½ teaspoon salt
¼ teaspoon pepper
⅛ teaspoon ground red pepper (cayenne)
12 cloves garlic
3 slices lemon, cut in half
2 large tomatoes, seeded and coarsely chopped
2 large onions, chopped (about 2 cups)
3 cups hot cooked couscous

Heat oven to 325°. Mix all ingredients except couscous in ungreased 3-quart casserole. Cover and bake 2 hours to 2 hours 30 minutes or until beef is very tender. Serve over couscous.

6 servings

PER SERVING: Calories 575; Protein 36 g; Carbohydrate 77 g; Fat 7 g; Cholesterol 70 mg; Sodium 390 mg

Hungarian Beef Goulash

Goulash gets a special spicy quality from Hungarian paprika, considered by many to be the superior variety. Paprika is a powder made by grinding sweet pepper pods, and its flavor ranges from mild to pungent, its color from orange-red to deep red. You'll find the more pungent varieties in markets that stack imported foods.

1 tablespoon vegetable oil
1½-pound beef boneless chuck, tip or round, cut into ¾-inch cubes
3 cups chopped onions (about 3 large)
2 cups water
1 tablespoon paprika
2 teaspoons salt
1 teaspoon beef bouillon granules
½ teaspoon caraway seed
¼ teaspoon pepper
1 clove garlic, chopped
1 can (8 ounces) whole tomatoes, undrained
2 medium potatoes, cut into 1½-inch pieces
2 green bell peppers, cut into 1-inch pieces

Heat oil in Dutch oven or 12-inch skillet. Cook beef about 15 minutes, stirring occasionally, until brown; drain. Stir in remaining ingredients except potatoes and bell peppers; break up tomatoes. Heat to boiling, reduce heat. Cover and simmer 1 hour.

Stir in potatoes. Cover and simmer about 30 minutes or until beef and potatoes are tender. Stir in bell peppers. Cover and simmer 8 to 10 minutes or until tender. Serve in soup bowls with French bread for dipping into hot broth if desired. **6 servings**

PER SERVING: Calories 270; Protein 27 g; Carbohydrate 22 g; Fat 8 g; Cholesterol 70 mg; Sodium 920 mg

Meat Loaf

¾ **pound extra-lean ground beef**
¾ **pound ground turkey**
½ **cup regular oats**
½ **cup tomato puree**
¼ **cup chopped onion (about 1 small)**
2 **tablespoons chopped fresh parsley or**
   2 **teaspoons dried parsley flakes**
½ **teaspoon Italian seasoning**
½ **teaspoon salt**
¼ **teaspoon pepper**
1 **clove garlic, finely chopped**

Heat oven to 350°. Mix all ingredients thoroughly. Press mixture evenly in ungreased loaf pan, 8½ × 4½ × 2½ or 9 × 5 × 3 inches, or shape into loaf in ungreased rectangular pan, 13 × 9 × 2 inches. Bake uncovered 1 hour 15 minutes to 1 hour 30 minutes or until center is no longer pink.   **6 servings**

PER SERVING: Calories 215; Protein 29 g; Carbohydrate 6 g; Fat 7 g; Cholesterol 80 mg; Sodium 340 mg

Extra-Easy Beef Fajitas

6 **ounces thinly sliced cooked lean beef**
1 **tablespoon lime juice**
¼ **teaspoon garlic powder**
¼ **teaspoon red pepper flakes**
8 **eight-inch flour tortillas**
4 **medium green or red bell peppers**
1 **medium onion**
1 **cup canned pinto beans, rinsed and**
   drained
½ **cup plain nonfat yogurt**
½ **cup salsa**

Heat oven to 325°. Cut beef into ½-inch strips. Mix beef, lime juice, garlic powder and red pepper flakes. Wrap tortillas in aluminum foil. Heat in oven about 15 minutes or until warm. Mean-while, cut bell peppers into strips. Cut onion into slices; separate into rings.

Spray 10-inch nonstick skillet with nonstick cooking spray; heat until hot. Cook and stir onion in skillet 1 minute. Add peppers; cook and stir 2 minutes. Add beef mixture and beans; cook and stir about 3 minutes or until beans are hot. Fill warm tortillas with hot beef mixture. Serve with yogurt and salsa.   **4 servings**

PER SERVING: Calories 335; Protein 21 g; Carbohydrate 54 g; Fat 5 g; Cholesterol 30 mg; Sodium 560 mg

Meat Tips

- Rather than make floury sauces and gravies, just reduce pan juices to the desired consistency and concentration of flavor. Remove the fat from meat cooking juices: Pour the juices into a fat separator (which has a spout coming from the bottom of the container—below the fat line, because fat rises to the liquid surface) or, refrigerate, then skim off congealed fat.

- Select lean cuts of meat and trim off all visible fat before cooking.

- Avoid frying meats, a cooking method that only adds fat to a fatty situation. Use nonstick cookware so less added fat is needed in cooking.

- Meat roasted on a rack can't cook in (and reabsorb) its own fat.

- Baste meats with their own juices, broth, or water rather than margarine.

- Marinades don't have to be oil based. Use flavored vinegars, herbs and spices.

- When buying ground beef, choose extra-lean.

Sauerbraten Meatballs and Noodles

Sauerbraten Meatballs and Noodles

1 pound lean ground beef or pork
⅓ cup crushed gingersnaps (about 6 gingersnaps)
½ cup finely chopped onion (about 1 medium)
¼ cup water
½ teaspoon salt
¼ teaspoon pepper
6 ounces uncooked egg noodles or spaetzle (about 3 cups)
1 cup beef broth
¼ cup apple cider vinegar
¼ cup crushed gingersnaps (about 4 gingersnaps)
1 tablespoon sugar
2 tablespoons raisins

Heat oven to 400°. Mix ground beef, ⅓ cup gingersnaps, the onion, water, salt and pepper. Shape mixture into 24 meatballs. Spray rack in broiler pan with nonstick cooking spray. Place meatballs on rack. Bake uncovered 20 to 25 minutes or until done and light brown.

Cook noodles as directed on package; drain. Mix remaining ingredients except raisins in 1½-quart saucepan. Cook over medium heat, stirring constantly, until mixture thickens and boils. Stir in raisins and meatballs. Heat until hot. Serve over noodles.   **6 servings**

PER SERVING: Calories 300; Protein 24 g; Carbohydrate 34 g; Fat 7 g; Cholesterol 85 mg; Sodium 480 mg

Curried Beef with Fruit

1 package (8 ounces) mixed dried fruit
2½ cups boiling water
3 teaspoons curry powder
½ teaspoon salt
2 cloves garlic, finely chopped
2 tablespoons margarine or butter
2 tablespoons cornstarch
¼ cup orange juice
¾ cup orange juice
3 cups cut-up cooked roast beef
6 green onions, cut into 1-inch pieces
3 cups hot cooked rice
⅓ cup slivered almonds

Remove pits from prunes. Pour boiling water over fruit; let stand. Cook curry powder, salt and garlic in margarine in 3-quart saucepan over medium heat 5 minutes, stirring occasionally. Mix cornstarch and ¼ cup orange juice. Stir cornstarch mixture, ¾ cup orange juice and the fruit (with liquid) into curry mixture. Heat to boiling, stirring constantly. Boil and stir 1 minute. Stir in beef and onions; heat until hot. Serve over rice. Sprinkle with almonds.   **6 servings**

PER SERVING: Calories 480; Protein 28 g; Carbohydrate 66 g; Fat 12 g; Cholesterol 65 mg; Sodium 670 mg

Beef-Vegetable Stew with Barley

Beef-Vegetable Stew with Barley

1 pound beef stew meat, cut into 1-inch
    pieces
1 tablespoon vegetable oil
1 cup dry red wine or beef broth
1 teaspoon chopped fresh or ¼ teaspoon
    dried rosemary leaves, crushed
¼ teaspoon pepper
1 clove garlic, finely chopped
1 can (10½ ounces) beef broth
1 can (14½ ounces) whole tomatoes,
    undrained
½ cup uncooked barley
2 cups sliced carrots (about 2 medium)
1 cup broccoli flowerets
1 medium onion, cut into wedges
4 ounces medium mushrooms, cut into
    halves

Cook beef in oil in 4-quart Dutch oven, stirring
occasionally, until brown. Stir in wine, rosemary,
pepper, garlic, broth and tomatoes; break up tomatoes. Heat to boiling; reduce heat. Cover and
simmer 1 hour.

Stir in barley. Cover and simmer about 30 minutes or until beef is almost tender. Stir in remaining ingredients. Cover and simmer about 20
minutes or until vegetables are tender.

4 servings

PER SERVING: Calories 290; Protein 23 g; Carbohydrate 23 g; Fat 9 g; Cholesterol 55 mg; Sodium 330 mg

Harvest Beef Stew

A hearty, satisfying stew.

2 pounds beef stew meat, cut into 1-inch
    cubes
⅓ cup quick-cooking tapioca
1 tablespoon chopped fresh or 1 tea-
    spoon dried basil leaves
1 tablespoon cumin seed
1 teaspoon salt
4 medium carrots, cut into 1-inch pieces
4 cloves garlic, finely chopped
2 medium onions, cut into eighths
2 cans (16 ounces) tomatoes, undrained
2 ears fresh corn, cut into fourths,* or 1
    package (10 ounces) frozen whole ker-
    nel corn
8 small new potatoes (about 1 pound),
    cut in half
2 small zucchini, thinly sliced

Heat oven to 325°. Mix all ingredients except
corn, potatoes and zucchini in Dutch oven;
break up tomatoes. Cover and bake 2 hours 30
minutes, stirring 2 or 3 times during the first 1
hour 30 minutes. Stir corn and potatoes into
stew. Cover and bake 1 hour to 1 hour 30 minutes longer or until beef and vegetables are
tender. Stir in zucchini. Cover and let stand 10
minutes. **8 servings**

*4 ears frozen corn, thawed and cut in half, can be substi-
tuted for the fresh corn.

PER SERVING: Calories 305; Protein 28 g; Carbohydrate 37 g; Fat 6 g; Cholesterol 70 mg; Sodium 530 mg

Caribbean Pork Tenderloin

The plantain, a less-sweet cousin of the banana, is a principal starch in the Caribbean.

2 lean pork tenderloins, about ½ pound each
1 teaspoon grated orange peel
½ cup orange juice
2 tablespoons lime juice
2 tablespoons chopped cilantro
½ teaspoon cracked black pepper
2 cloves garlic, cut in half
1 teaspoon cornstarch
¼ teaspoon salt
1 teaspoon vegetable oil
1 large ripe plantain, cut into ¼-inch slices

Trim fat from pork tenderloin. Cut pork across grain into ⅛-inch slices. (For ease in cutting, partially freeze pork, about 1 hour 30 minutes.) Mix orange peel, orange juice, lime juice, cilantro, pepper and garlic in large glass or plastic bowl. Stir in pork. Cover and refrigerate 30 minutes.

Remove pork from marinade and drain. Stir cornstarch and salt into marinade; reserve. Heat oil in 10-inch nonstick skillet over medium-high heat. Cook and stir pork in oil about 4 minutes or until no longer pink. Stir in plantain; cook and stir until brown. Stir in marinade mixture. Heat to boiling, stirring constantly. Boil and stir 1 minute. **4 servings**

PER SERVING: Calories 175; Protein 17 g; Carbohydrate 20 g; Fat 3 g; Cholesterol 50 mg; Sodium 175 mg

Harvest Pork Tenderloins

¾-pound lean pork tenderloin, cut into 4 slices
2 teaspoons olive or vegetable oil
½ cup chopped onion (about 1 medium)
2 teaspoons chopped fresh or ½ teaspoon dried rosemary leaves, crushed
¼ teaspoon salt
⅛ teaspoon pepper
1 clove garlic, finely chopped
2 cups cubed acorn or butternut squash
1 cup chopped apple (about 1 medium)
½ cup apple cider or apple juice
2 tablespoons raisins

Pound pork tenderloin slices until ½ inch thick. Heat oil in 10-inch nonstick skillet over medium heat. Cook pork, turning once, about 12 minutes or until done. Remove pork from skillet; keep warm.

Cook onion, rosemary, salt, pepper and garlic in skillet over medium heat about 3 minutes, stirring occasionally, until onion is tender. Stir in remaining ingredients. Top with pork. Reduce heat to low. Cover and cook about 10 minutes or until squash is tender. **4 servings**

PER SERVING: Calories 215; Protein 20 g; Carbohydrate 21 g; Fat 6 g; Cholesterol 60 mg; Sodium 190 mg

Gingered Pork with Peaches

1-pound pork tenderloin
1 tablespoon vegetable oil
2 tablespoons soy sauce
2 teaspoons finely chopped gingerroot or
  1 teaspoon ground ginger
2 teaspoons cornstarch
⅛ teaspoon pepper
2 cloves garlic, finely chopped
2 tablespoons vegetable oil
½ cup slivered almonds
½ cup chicken broth
3 medium peaches, peeled and sliced*
6 green onions, cut into 1-inch pieces
3 cups hot cooked rice

Trim fat from pork tenderloin. Cut pork with grain into 2-inch strips. Cut strips across grain into ¼-inch slices. (For ease in cutting, partially freeze pork, about 1 hour 30 minutes.) Toss pork with 1 tablespoon oil, the soy sauce, gingerroot, cornstarch, pepper and garlic.

Heat 2 tablespoons oil in 10-inch skillet over medium-high heat until hot. Rotate skillet until oil covers bottom. Stir-fry pork and almonds 6 to 8 minutes or until pork is brown. Add chicken broth. Stir about 1 minute or until thickened. Add peaches and onions. Stir about 3 minutes or until peaches are hot. Serve over rice.

6 servings

*1 package (16 ounces) frozen sliced peaches, thawed and drained, can be substituted for the fresh peaches.

PER SERVING: Calories 315; Protein 21 g; Carbohydrate 34 g; Fat 10 g; Cholesterol 50 mg; Sodium 830 mg

Ham and Zucchini

You can substitute smoked turkey for the ham if you like.

1 tablespoon reduced-calorie margarine
1 medium onion, thinly sliced
3 cups cut-up fully cooked smoked ham
  (about 1 pound)
4 small zucchini (about 1 pound), cut
  into julienne strips
1 green bell pepper, cut into ¼-inch
  strips
⅛ teaspoon pepper
¼ cup low-fat sour cream
¼ cup plain nonfat yogurt
1 teaspoon poppy seed
3 cups hot cooked noodles or rice

Heat margarine in 10-inch nonstick skillet. Cook onion, stirring occasionally, until softened. Stir in ham, zucchini, bell pepper and pepper. Cover and cook over medium heat about 8 minutes, stirring occasionally, until vegetables are crisp-tender.

Stir in sour cream, yogurt and poppy seed. Heat just until hot. Serve with noodles.

6 servings

PER SERVING: Calories 270; Protein 22 g; Carbohydrate 29 g; Fat 7 g; Cholesterol 50 mg; Sodium 980 mg

Spicy Black Bean and Pork Stew

4 cups water
½ cup dried black beans (about 4 ounces)
2 ancho chiles
¾-pound lean pork boneless shoulder
1½ cups chopped seeded peeled tomatoes (about 2 large)
½ cup chopped onion (about 1 medium)
½ cup dry red wine or chicken broth
1 tablespoon chopped fresh or 1 teaspoon dried sage leaves
1 tablespoon chopped fresh or 1 teaspoon dried marjoram leaves
½ teaspoon salt
½ teaspoon ground cumin
¼ teaspoon ground cinnamon
1 clove garlic, finely chopped
2 cups 1-inch cubes peeled butternut squash
1 medium red bell pepper, cut into 1-inch pieces
2 tablespoons chopped cilantro

Heat water, beans and chiles to boiling in Dutch oven. Boil uncovered 2 minutes; remove from heat. Cover and let stand 1 hour. Remove chiles; reserve. Heat beans to boiling; reduce heat. Simmer covered for 1 hour.

Seed and coarsely chop chiles. Trim fat from pork shoulder. Cut pork into 1-inch cubes. Stir pork, chiles and remaining ingredients except squash, bell pepper and cilantro into beans. Heat to boiling; reduce heat. Cover and simmer 30 minutes, stirring occasionally. Stir in squash. Cover and simmer 30 minutes, stirring occasionally, until squash is tender. Stir in bell pepper and cilantro. Cover and simmer about 5 minutes or until bell pepper is crisp-tender.

4 servings

PER SERVING: Calories 315; Protein 22 g; Carbohydrate 34 g; Fat 7 g; Cholesterol 50 mg; Sodium 330 mg

Scalloped Potatoes and Ham

2 tablespoons reduced-calorie margarine
3 tablespoons all-purpose flour
½ teaspoon dry mustard
¼ teaspoon salt
⅛ teaspoon pepper
2 cups skim milk
3 cups thinly sliced peeled potatoes (about 3 medium)
1 cup diced fully cooked smoked extra-lean ham (about 6 ounces)
¼ cup finely chopped onion (about 1 small)

Heat oven to 350°. Spray 1½-quart casserole with nonstick cooking spray. Heat margarine in 1½-quart saucepan over medium heat. Stir in flour, mustard, salt and pepper. Cook, stirring constantly, until margarine is absorbed. Gradually stir in milk. Heat to boiling, stirring constantly. Boil and stir 1 minute.

Layer one-third of the potatoes, half of the ham, half of the onion and one-third of the sauce in casserole; repeat. Top with remaining potatoes and sauce. Cover and bake 30 minutes. Uncover and bake about 40 minutes or until potatoes are tender. Let stand 5 to 10 minutes before serving.

4 servings

PER SERVING: Calories 180; Protein 14 g; Carbohydrate 15 g; Fat 6 g; Cholesterol 15 mg; Sodium 720 mg

Spicy Black Bean and Pork Stew

Lamb Paprikash

**1-pound lean lamb boneless shoulder or
   leg**
1 can (6 ounces) tomato paste
**1 can (16 ounces) tomatoes, drained (re-
   serve ⅓ cup liquid)**
2 tablespoons paprika
**1 tablespoon chopped fresh or 1½ tea-
   spoons dried oregano leaves**
¼ teaspoon pepper
1 medium onion, thinly sliced
**1 medium green bell pepper, cut into
   ¼-inch strips**
2 cloves garlic, finely chopped
8 ounces mushrooms, cut into fourths
3 cups hot cooked noodles

Heat oven to 325°. Trim fat from lamb shoulder; cut lamb into ½-inch cubes. Cook and stir lamb over medium heat in 4-quart nonstick Dutch oven until brown, about 5 minutes. Stir in tomato paste. Mix in reserved tomato liquid and the remaining ingredients except noodles; break up tomatoes. Cover and bake, stirring once, until lamb is tender, 45 to 55 minutes. Serve over noodles. **6 servings**

PER SERVING: Calories 275; Protein 22 g; Carbohydrate 34 g; Fat 6 g; Cholesterol 80 mg; Sodium 180 mg

If you like mayonnaise and salad dressing, but are confused by the choices available, here's an easy lesson:

- Regular mayonnaise or salad dressing contains 60 to 100 calories per tablespoon.

- Reduced-calorie, light or "lite" mayonnaise contains 20 to 50 calories per tablespoon.

- Regular, cholesterol-free mayonnaise and salad dressing has 60 to 100 calories per tablespoon but does not contain cholesterol because the egg yolk has been omitted.

- Reduced-calorie, light or "lite" cholesterol-free mayonnaise contains 20 to 50 calories per tablespoon and also has no cholesterol.

- Vinaigrette-type bottled salad dressings are made from vegetable oils and are cholesterol-free but can contain 45 to 100 calories and 4 to 9 grams of fat per tablespoon. The total oil content has been cut in the reduced-calorie counterparts, which in many cases are oil-free. Recipes for salad dressings typically use 3 parts oil to 1 part vinegar. Try using 1 part oil to 1 part vinegar. Mild vinegars with flavorings such as balsamic or raspberry reduced tartness.

- Creamy bottled salad dressings vary widely in fat content, cholesterol and calorie counts. Many bottled dressings average 60 to 80 calories and 6 to 8 grams of fat per tablespoon, while the reduced-calorie versions are one-quarter to one-half that amount.

Minty Lamb Stir-fry

A quick and different stir-fry.

6 ounces uncooked angel hair pasta
½ cup mashed peeled kiwifruit (about 2 medium)
1 tablespoon chopped fresh or 1 teaspoon dried mint leaves, crushed
1 teaspoon cornstarch
¼ teaspoon salt
1 tablespoon vegetable oil
¾-pound lean lamb boneless shoulder or leg, cut into 2 × ¼-inch strips
1 clove garlic, finely chopped
1 cup julienne strips carrots (about 2 medium)
1 cup julienne strips zucchini (about 5 ounces)

Cook pasta as directed on package; drain. Mix kiwifruit, mint, cornstarch and salt.

Heat oil in 10-inch nonstick skillet over medium-high heat. Stir-fry lamb and garlic about 3 minutes or until lamb is no longer pink. Add carrots and zucchini; stir-fry 2 minutes. Add kiwifruit mixture; stir-fry 1 minute. Serve over pasta.

4 servings

PER SERVING: Calories 320; Protein 27 g; Carbohydrate 36 g; Fat 8 g; Cholesterol 105 mg; Sodium 210 mg

Lamb Patties with Fresh Mint Sauce

Fresh Mint Sauce (below)
1 pound lean ground lamb
⅔ cup soft bread crumbs
⅓ cup dry red wine or chicken broth
½ teaspoon salt
¼ teaspoon dried rosemary leaves, crushed
2 small cloves garlic, finely chopped

Prepare Fresh Mint Sauce. Set oven control to broil. Mix remaining ingredients. Shape lamb mixture into 4 patties, each about 1 inch thick. Place patties on rack sprayed with nonstick cooking spray in broiler pan. Broil with tops about 3 inches from heat, until of desired doneness, 5 to 7 minutes on each side for medium. Serve with Fresh Mint Sauce. Garnish with mint leaves and sliced kiwifruit if desired.

4 servings

Fresh Mint Sauce

¼ cup mashed peeled kiwifruit (about 1 medium)
1 tablespoon chopped fresh or ½ teaspoon dried mint leaves, crushed
2 teaspoons sugar
2 teaspoons lime juice

Mix all ingredients.

PER SERVING: Calories 260; Protein 29 g; Carbohydrate 16 g; Fat 7 g; Cholesterol 95 mg; Sodium 460 mg

Chocolate-Orange Angel Food Cake (page 84)

5

Delicious Desserts

Baked Apples

Baked apples are a satisfying dessert, and with the microwave, you can make them in a snap.

4 large unpeeled apples (Rome, Beauty, Golden Delicious, greening)
2 to 4 tablespoons granulated or packed brown sugar
4 teaspoons margarine or butter
½ teaspoon ground cinnamon

Heat oven to 375°. Core apples. Peel 1-inch strip of skin around middle of each apple, or peel upper half of each to prevent splitting. Place apples in ungreased baking dish. Place 1 teaspoon to 1 tablespoon sugar, 1 teaspoon margarine and ⅛ teaspoon cinnamon in center of each apple. Sprinkle with cinnamon. Pour water into baking dish until ¼ inch deep.

Bake 30 to 40 minutes or until tender when pierced with fork. (Time will vary with size and variety of apple.) Spoon syrup in dish over apples several times during baking if desired. **4 servings**

MICROWAVE DIRECTIONS: Prepare apples as directed—except omit water. Place each apple in 10-ounce custard cups or individual casseroles. Microwave uncovered on high 5 to 10 minutes, rotating cups ½ turn after 3 minutes, until apples are tender when pierced with fork.

BAKED MINCEMEAT APPLES: Omit sugar, margarine and cinnamon. Fill each apple with 1 to 2 tablespoons prepared mincemeat.

PER SERVING: Calories 165;   Protein 0 g;   Carbohydrate 34 g; Fat 4 g; Cholesterol 0 mg; Sodium 45 mg

Creamy Peach Freeze, Capped Fig Cookies (page 91)

Creamy Peach Freeze

This fresh dessert is not only fat-free, it also has no cholesterol.

½ **cup cholesterol-free egg product**
⅔ **cup sugar**
1½ **cups skim milk**
¼ **teaspoon salt**
2 **cups mashed peeled peaches (4 to 5 medium)***
2 **teaspoons vanilla**
2 **containers (8 ounces each) peach non-fat yogurt**

Mix egg product, sugar, milk and salt in 2-quart saucepan. Cook over medium heat, stirring constantly, just until bubbles appear around edge. Pour into chilled large metal bowl. Refrigerate 1 hour 30 minutes to 2 hours, stirring occasionally, until at room temperature.

Stir peaches, vanilla and yogurt into milk mixture. Pour into 1-quart ice-cream freezer and freeze according to manufacturer's directions. **8 servings**

*1 package (16 ounces) frozen sliced peaches, thawed and mashed, can be substituted for the fresh peaches.

MICROWAVE DIRECTIONS: Place milk in 4-cup microwavable measure. Microwave uncovered on high 2 to 3 minutes or until very warm. Beat in egg product, sugar and salt. Microwave uncovered on medium-high (70%) 3 to 4 minutes, stirring every minute, until thickened. Continue as directed.

PER SERVING: Calories 130; Protein 6 g; Carbohydrate 26 g; Fat 0 g; Cholesterol 0 mg; Sodium 150 mg

Spicy Fruit Compote

1 **two-inch cinnamon stick**
6 **whole cloves**
¼ **cup sugar**
½ **cup port, sweet red wine or apple juice**
½ **cup water**
2 **tablespoons lemon juice**
1 **package (11 ounces) mixed dried fruit**
2 **bananas, sliced**

Tie cinnamon stick and cloves in cheesecloth bag. Heat cheesecloth bag, sugar, port, water and lemon juice to boiling in 2-quart saucepan. Stir in dried fruit. Heat to boiling; reduce heat. Simmer uncovered 10 to 15 minutes, stirring occasionally, until fruit is plump and tender. Refrigerate uncovered about 3 hours, stirring occasionally, until chilled.

Remove cheesecloth bag. Stir bananas into fruit mixture until coated with syrup. Drain fruit, reserving syrup. Serve fruit with some of the syrup. Serve with low-fat sour cream or plain yogurt if desired. **6 servings**

PER SERVING: Calories 220; Protein 1 g; Carbohydrate 58 g; Fat 0 g; Cholesterol 0 mg; Sodium 10 mg

Mango with Passion Fruit

**1 large mango (about 1 pound), thinly
sliced**
8 pitted dates, cut in half
1 passion fruit
**½ cup vanilla yogurt or low-fat sour
cream**

Arrange mango and dates on 4 dessert plates.
Cut passion fruit in half and scoop out center.
Mix passion fruit and yogurt. Serve with fruit.

4 servings

PER SERVING: Calories 110; Protein 2 g; Carbohydrate 23 g; Fat 1 g; Cholesterol 0 mg; Sodium 20 mg

Frozen Fresh Berry Yogurt

2 pints strawberries or raspberries
½ cup sugar
8 cups vanilla yogurt

Mash strawberries with sugar. Stir into yogurt.
Pour into 2-quart ice-cream freezer and freeze
according to manufacturer's directions.*

22 servings

*A 1-quart ice-cream freezer can be used. Divide ingredients
in half.

FROZEN BANANA YOGURT: Substitute 3 cups
mashed banana (about 8 medium) for the
strawberries.

PER SERVINGS: Calories 110; Protein 3 g; Carbohydrate 21 g; Fat 2 g; Cholesterol 0 mg; Sodium 55 mg

Peach Sorbet with Pineapple

**1 package (16 ounces) frozen unsweet-
ened peach slices**
¼ cup unsweetened apple juice
6 slices pineapple,* ½ inch thick

Place half of the peaches and 2 tablespoons
apple juice at a time in food processor. Cover
and process until smooth. Freeze at least 2
hours or until icy. Scoop or spoon over pineapple slices. (If sorbet becomes too firm to scoop,
remove from freezer and refrigerate for about 1
hour before serving.) **6 servings**

*6 canned pineapple slices in juice, drained, can be substi-
tuted for fresh pineapple slices.

PER SERVING: Calories 125; Protein 1 g; Carbohydrate 30 g; Fat 0 g; Cholesterol 0 mg; Sodium 5 mg

Fruit Fun

- A great variety of fresh fruits are now
  available to us. Choose fruits at their
  seasonal peak for the fullest flavors and
  the most economical pieces.

- Fruits can be served as snacks or as ap-
  pealing desserts. Serve whole and uncut,
  cut up and mixed or baked in delicious
  cobblers.

- Orchard fruits, citrus fruits and even
  those that used to be considered exotic,
  such as kiwifruit, mangoes and papayas,
  are now close to staples. Even unusual
  fruits such as carambolas, tamarinds and
  prickly pears are becoming easy to find.

- Canned and frozen fruits may be used
  in many recipes that call for fresh fruits
  not in season.

Fresh Blueberry Cobbler

½ cup sugar
1 tablespoon cornstarch
4 cups blueberries
1 teaspoon lemon juice
3 tablespoons shortening
1 cup all-purpose flour*
1 tablespoon sugar
1½ teaspoons baking powder
½ teaspoon salt
½ cup milk

Heat oven to 400°. Mix ½ cup sugar and the cornstarch in 2-quart saucepan. Stir in blueberries and lemon juice. Cook, stirring constantly, until mixture thickens and boils. Boil and stir 1 minute. Pour into ungreased 2-quart casserole; keep blueberry mixture hot in oven.

Cut shortening into flour, 1 tablespoon sugar, the baking powder and salt until mixture resembles fine crumbs. Stir in milk. Drop dough by 6 spoonfuls onto hot blueberry mixture.

Bake 25 to 30 minutes or until topping is golden brown. Serve warm.   **6 servings**

*If using self-rising flour, omit baking powder and salt.

FRESH CHERRY COBBLER: Substitute 4 cups pitted and red tart cherries for the blueberries. Increase sugar in cherry mixture to 1¼ cups and cornstarch to 3 tablespoons. Add ¼ teaspoon ground cinnamon with the cornstarch. Substitute ¼ teaspoon almond extract for the lemon juice.

FRESH PEACH COBBLER: Substitute 4 cups sliced peaches (about 6 medium) for the blueberries. Add ¼ teaspoon ground cinnamon with the cornstarch.

PER SERVING: Calories 265; Protein 3 g; Carbohydrate 49 g; Fat 7 g; Cholesterol 0 mg; Sodium 300 mg

Bread Pudding with Brown Sugar Meringue

1½ cups lukewarm skim milk
1 egg
2 egg yolks
¼ cup packed brown sugar
½ teaspoon ground cinnamon
1 teaspoon vanilla
¼ teaspoon salt
3 cups toasted bread cubes (4 slices bread)
Brown Sugar Meringue (below)

Heat oven to 350°. Spray 1½-quart soufflé dish or casserole with nonstick cooking spray. Mix milk, egg and egg yolks, brown sugar, cinnamon, vanilla and salt in large bowl; stir in bread cubes. Bake uncovered until knife inserted 1 inch from edge comes out almost clean, 30 to 35 minutes.

Prepare Brown Sugar Meringue; spoon onto hot bread pudding. Spread over top, mounding to form peaks and carefully sealing meringue to edge of dish to prevent shrinking or weeping. Bake until peaks are golden brown, 12 to 15 minutes. Serve warm or cold. Refrigerate any remaining pudding.   **6 servings**

Brown Sugar Meringue

2 egg whites
¼ teaspoon cream of tartar
3 tablespoons packed brown sugar
½ teaspoon vanilla

Beat egg whites and cream of tartar in small bowl until foamy. Beat in brown sugar, 1 tablespoon at a time; continue beating until stiff and glossy. Do not underbeat. Beat in vanilla.

PER SERVING: Calories 155; Protein 6 g; Carbohydrate 26 g; Fat 3 g; Cholesterol 115 mg; Sodium 270 mg

Chocolate Swirl Cheesecake with Raspberry Topping

Chocolate Swirl Cheesecake with Raspberry Topping

Thick yogurt helps make this luscious cheesecake low in fat.

4 chocolate wafers, crushed (about ¼ cup)
2 cups Thick Yogurt (page 15)
1 package (8 ounces) Neufchâtel cheese, softened
⅔ cup sugar
¼ cup skim milk
2 tablespoons all-purpose flour
2 teaspoons vanilla
3 egg whites or ½ cup cholesterol-free egg product
1 tablespoon cocoa
1 teaspoon chocolate extract
Raspberry Topping (right)

Heat oven to 300°. Spray springform pan, 9 × 3 inches, with nonstick cooking spray. Sprinkle chocolate wafer crumbs on bottom of pan. Beat Thick Yogurt and cheese in medium bowl on medium speed until smooth. Add sugar, milk, flour, vanilla and egg whites. Beat on medium speed about 2 minutes or until smooth.

Place 1 cup batter in small bowl. Beat in cocoa and chocolate extract until blended. Carefully spread vanilla batter over crumbs in pan. Drop chocolate batter by spoonfuls onto vanilla batter. Swirl through batter with metal spatula for marbled effect, being careful not to touch bottom.

Bake 1 hour. Turn off oven; leave cheesecake in oven 30 minutes. Remove from oven; cool 15 minutes. Prepare Raspberry Topping; spread over cheesecake. Cover and refrigerate at least 3 hours. Or spoon Raspberry Topping over individual servings of chilled cheesecake.

12 servings

Raspberry Topping

1 package (10 ounces) frozen raspberries, thawed, drained and juice reserved
¼ cup sugar
2 tablespoons cornstarch

Add enough water to reserved juice to measure 1¼ cups. Mix sugar and cornstarch in 1½-quart saucepan. Stir in juice mixture and raspberries. Heat to boiling over medium heat, stirring frequently. Boil and stir 1 minute; cool.

PER SERVING: Calories 195; Protein 6 g; Carbohydrate 32 g; Fat 5 g; Cholesterol 15 mg; Sodium 150 mg

Angel Food Cake

Fat-free Angel Food Cake is a lovely ending to a meal.

1½ **cups powdered sugar**
1 **cup cake flour**
1½ **cups egg whites (about 12)**
1½ **teaspoons cream of tartar**
1 **cup granulated sugar**
1½ **teaspoons vanilla**
½ **teaspoon almond extract**
¼ **teaspoon salt**

Move oven rack to lowest position. Heat oven to 375°. Mix powdered sugar and flour. Beat egg whites and cream of tartar in medium bowl on medium speed until foamy. Beat in granulated sugar on high speed, 2 tablespoons at a time, adding vanilla, almond extract and salt with the last addition of sugar. Continue beating until stiff and glossy. Do not underbeat.

Sprinkle sugar-flour mixture, ¼ cup at a time, over meringue, folding in just until sugar-flour mixture disappears. Push batter into ungreased tube pan, 10 × 4 inches. Gently cut through batter with metal spatula.

Bake 30 to 35 minutes or until cracks in cake feel dry and top springs back when touched lightly. Immediately invert pan onto glass bottle or metal funnel. Let hang about 2 hours or until cake is completely cool. Remove from pan.

16 servings

COCONUT ANGEL FOOD CAKE: Fold in 1 cup shredded coconut, ½ cup at a time, after folding in sugar-flour mixture.

PER SERVING: Calories 130; Protein 3 g; Carbohydrate 29 g; Fat 0 g; Cholesterol 0 mg; Sodium 80 mg

Chocolate-Orange Angel Food Cake

1½ **cups powdered sugar**
¾ **cup cake flour**
¼ **cup cocoa**
1½ **cups egg whites (about 12)**
1½ **teaspoons cream of tartar**
1 **cup granulated sugar**
¼ **teaspoon salt**
3 **cups orange sherbet, softened**

Move oven rack to lowest position. Heat oven to 375°. Sift together powdered sugar, flour and cocoa. Beat egg whites and cream of tartar in large bowl on medium speed until foamy. Beat in granulated sugar, 2 tablespoons at a time, on high speed, adding salt with the last addition of sugar. Continue beating until stiff and glossy. Do not underbeat.

Sprinkle cocoa mixture, ¼ cup at a time, over meringue, folding in just until cocoa mixture disappears. Spread batter in ungreased tube pan, 10 × 4 inches. Gently cut through batter with metal spatula.

Bake 30 to 35 minutes or until cracks feel dry and top springs back when touched lightly. Immediately invert pan onto glass bottle or metal funnel. Let hang about 2 hours or until cake is completely cool. Remove from pan.

Slice off top of cake about 1 inch down; set aside. Cut down into cake 1 inch from outer edge and 1 inch from edge of hole, leaving substantial "walls" on each side. Remove cake within cuts with curved knife or spoon, being careful to leave a base of cake 1 inch thick. Spoon sherbet into cake cavity; smooth top. Replace top of cake. Cover and freeze about 3 hours or until firm. **16 servings**

PER SERVING: Calories 175; Protein 3 g; Carbohydrate 39 g; Fat 1 g; Cholesterol 5 mg; Sodium 85 mg

Gingerbread with Orange Sauce

This ginger loaf is tender and moist. Orange is a delicious accompaniment.

1 cup all-purpose flour
¼ cup molasses
¼ cup hot water
2 tablespoons packed brown sugar
2 tablespoons shortening
½ teaspoon baking soda
½ teaspoon ground ginger
½ teaspoon ground cinnamon
⅛ teaspoon salt
1 egg white
Orange Sauce (right)

Heat oven to 325°. Spray loaf pan, 8½ × 4½ × 2½ inches, with nonstick cooking spray. Beat all ingredients except Orange Sauce on low speed 30 seconds, scraping bowl constantly. Beat on medium speed 3 minutes, scraping bowl occasionally. Pour into pan.

Bake until wooden pick inserted in center comes out clean, 30 to 35 minutes. Cool 10 minutes; remove from pan. Serve warm or cool with Orange Sauce. **8 servings**

Orange Sauce

3 tablespoons sugar
1 tablespoon cornstarch
1 cup water
1 tablespoon grated orange peel
1 tablespoon orange juice

Mix sugar and cornstarch in 1-quart saucepan. Gradually stir in water. Cook over medium heat until mixture thickens and boils, stirring constantly. Boil and stir 1 minute; remove from heat. Stir in orange peel and juice. Serve warm or cool.

PER SERVING: Calories 140; Protein 2 g; Carbohydrate 26 g; Fat 3 g; Cholesterol 0 mg; Sodium 120 mg

Dessert Tips

• Eat sugary desserts in moderation, but when it comes to fresh fruit you can really go to town. Enjoy it chopped, pureed, cold, hot, with sauces or without. Always use ripe fruit for the most flavorful results.

• When recipes call for such products as whipped cream, sour cream, cream cheese and ricotta cheese, use low-fat versions.

• Angel food cake is a perfect low-fat dessert. See our recipe (page 84).

• Fresh fruit ices and sherbets are made without eggs or cream, a boon to fat watchers. Combine luscious complementary fruits for seemingly endless variety.

Sacher Cake Roll

Sifted cocoa, rather than powdered sugar, is sprinkled on the towel before the cake is rolled, enhancing the deep chocolate flavor.

2 eggs
2 egg whites
¾ cup sugar
⅓ cup water
1 teaspoon vanilla
¾ cup all-purpose flour
3 tablespoons cocoa
1 teaspoon baking powder
¼ teaspoon salt
Cocoa
½ cup apricot preserves or jam
Chocolate Glaze (right)

Heat oven to 375°. Line jelly roll pan, 15½ × 10½ × 1 inch, with aluminum foil or waxed paper; spray with nonstick cooking spray. Beat eggs and egg whites in small bowl on high speed until very thick and lemon colored, about 5 minutes. Pour into medium bowl. Gradually beat in sugar. Beat in water and vanilla on low speed. Gradually beat in flour, 3 tablespoons cocoa, the baking powder and salt just until batter is smooth. Pour into pan.

Bake until wooden pick inserted in center comes out clean, 12 to 15 minutes. Immediately loosen cake from edges of pan; invert on towel sprinkled with cocoa. Carefully remove foil. Trim off stiff edges of cake if necessary. While hot, carefully roll cake and towel from narrow end. Cool on wire rack at least 30 minutes. Unroll cake; remove towel. Beat preserves with fork to soften; spread over top of cake. Roll up cake. Prepare Chocolate Glaze; immediately spread over cake roll.   **10 servings**

Chocolate Glaze

⅓ cup powdered sugar
1 tablespoon cocoa
1½ to 2½ teaspoons hot water
¼ teaspoon vanilla

Mix all ingredients until smooth and of desired consistency.

PER SERVING: Calories 180; Protein 3 g; Carbohydrate 38 g; Fat 2 g; Cholesterol 55 mg; Sodium 125 mg

Double Chocolate-Date Cake

Chocolate Chip Topping (below)
1 cup hot water
⅔ cup chopped dates
1⅔ cups all-purpose flour
1 cup packed brown sugar
¼ cup cocoa
1 teaspoon baking soda
¼ teaspoon salt
¼ cup vegetable oil
1 teaspoon cider vinegar
½ teaspoon vanilla

Heat oven to 350°. Prepare Chocolate Chip Topping; reserve. Pour hot water over dates in small bowl. Let stand 5 minutes. Drain dates, reserving water. Mix flour, brown sugar, cocoa, baking soda and salt in ungreased square pan, 8 × 8 × 2 inches. Stir in dates. Add enough water to date water to measure 1 cup. Stir water mixture and remaining ingredients into flour mixture. Sprinkle with topping. Bake 35 to 40 minutes or until wooden pick inserted in center comes out clean. **8 servings**

Chocolate Chip Topping

2 tablespoons miniature semisweet chocolate chips
2 tablespoons chopped walnuts
2 tablespoons packed brown sugar

Mix all ingredients.

PER SERVING: Calories 460; Protein 8 g; Carbohydrate 90 g; Fat 8 g; Cholesterol 0 mg; Sodium 220 mg

Lemon Meringue Cake with Strawberries

A meringue frosting makes this cake special. Egg product can't be used to make the meringue, as the fat will keep the egg whites from increasing in volume when beaten.

2 cups sliced strawberries
¼ cup sugar
1¼ cups all-purpose flour
1 cup sugar
¼ cup margarine, softened
½ cup skim milk
1½ teaspoons baking powder
1½ teaspoons grated lemon peel
1 teaspoon vanilla
¼ teaspoon salt
2 egg whites or ¼ cup cholesterol-free egg product
2 egg whites
½ cup sugar

Mix strawberries and ¼ cup sugar. Cover and refrigerate until serving time.

Heat oven to 350°. Spray square pan, 9 × 9 × 2 inches, with nonstick cooking spray. Beat flour, 1 cup sugar, the margarine, milk, baking powder, lemon peel, vanilla, salt and 2 egg whites in large bowl on low speed 30 seconds, scraping bowl constantly. Beat on high speed 2 minutes, scraping bowl occasionally. Pour into pan. Bake 25 to 30 minutes or until wooden pick inserted in center comes out clean.

Increase oven temperature to 400°. Beat 2 egg whites in medium bowl until foamy. Beat in ½ cup sugar, 1 tablespoon at a time. Continue beating until stiff and glossy. Spread over cake. Bake 8 to 10 minutes or until meringue is light brown; cool completely. Top each serving with strawberries. **9 servings**

PER SERVING: Calories 250; Protein 4 g; Carbohydrate 47 g; Fat 5 g; Cholesterol 0 mg; Sodium 220 mg

Blueberry-Lime Torte

Fresh blueberries and lime cream are mounded in a crisp, meringue shell.

Meringue Shell (right)
2 egg whites
1 egg
½ cup sugar
⅔ cup water
⅓ cup lime juice
1 envelope unflavored gelatin
1 tablespoon grated lime peel
4 egg whites
½ teaspoon cream of tartar
½ cup sugar
1½ cups blueberries

Bake Meringue shell; cool completely. Beat 2 egg whites and the egg in medium bowl until foamy. Mix ½ cup sugar, the water, lime juice and gelatin in 2-quart nonstick saucepan. Heat to boiling over medium heat, stirring constantly. Gradually stir at least half of the hot mixture into egg mixture. Stir into hot mixture in saucepan. Heat to boiling; remove from heat. Stir in lime peel. Place pan in bowl of ice and water, or refrigerate about 15 minutes, stirring occasionally, until mixture mounds when dropped from spoon.

Beat 4 egg whites and the cream of tartar in large bowl until foamy. Beat in ½ cup sugar, 1 tablespoon at a time. Continue beating until stiff and glossy. Do not underbeat. Fold in lime mixture. Place blueberries in shell. Spoon lime mixture over blueberries. Refrigerate 3 hours or until set. Garnish with lime twist and blueberries if desired. **8 servings**

Meringue Shell

3 egg whites
¼ teaspoon cream of tartar
¾ cup sugar

Heat oven to 275°. Line cookie sheet with cooking parchment paper or aluminum foil. Beat egg whites and cream of tartar in medium bowl until foamy. Beat in sugar, 1 tablespoon at a time. Continue beating until stiff and glossy. Do not underbeat. Shape meringue on cookie sheet into 9-inch circle with back of spoon, building up side. Bake 1 hour. Turn off oven. Leave meringue in oven with door closed 1 hour 30 minutes. Finish cooling meringue at room temperature.

PER SERVING: Calories 210; Protein 5 g; Carbohydrate 47 g; Fat 1 g; Cholesterol 25 mg; Sodium 70 mg

Poached Meringue with Apricot Sauce

Apricot Sauce (below)
Sugar
10 egg whites
½ teaspoon cream of tartar
1 cup sugar

Prepare Apricot Sauce. Grease 12-cup bundt cake pan and sprinkle with sugar. Heat oven to 350°. Beat egg whites and cream of tartar in large bowl until foamy. Beat in 1 cup sugar, 1 tablespoon at a time; continue beating until soft peaks form. Pour into pan. Gently cut through batter with metal spatula.

Place pan in shallow roasting pan on oven rack. Pour very hot water into roasting pan until 1 inch deep. Bake about 45 minutes or until top is golden brown and meringue is set.

Immediately loosen meringue from edges of pan. Invert onto heatproof serving plate. Cool 30 minutes. Refrigerate no longer than 24 hours. Cut meringue into wedges and serve with Apricot Sauce. **18 servings**

Apricot Sauce

1 package (6 ounces) dried apricots (about 1 cup)
2 cups water
2 to 3 tablespoons sugar
½ teaspoon ground cinnamon
1 teaspoon lemon juice

Heat apricots, water, sugar and cinnamon to boiling; reduce heat. Cover and simmer about 15 minutes or until apricots are tender. Place apricot mixture and lemon juice in blender. Cover a blend on medium-high speed about 15 seconds, stopping blender occasionally to scrape sides, until smooth. Stir in 1 to 2 tablespoons water, if necessary, until of sauce consistency. Refrigerate about 3 hours or until chilled.

PER SERVING: Calories 80; Protein 2 g; Carbohydrate 19 g; Fat 0 g; Cholesterol 0 mg; Sodium 35 mg

Coconut-Almond Macaroons

If you prefer, you can omit the candied cherries.

3 egg whites
¼ teaspoon cream of tartar
⅛ teaspoon salt
¾ cup sugar
¼ teaspoon almond extract
2 cups flaked coconut
About 12 candied cherries, each cut into fourths

Beat egg whites, cream of tartar and salt in small bowl until foamy. Beat in sugar, 1 tablespoon at a time; continue beating until stiff and glossy. Do not underbeat. Pour into medium bowl. Fold in almond extract and coconut.

Heat oven to 300°. Drop mixture by teaspoonfuls about 1 inch apart onto aluminum foil-covered cookie sheet. Place a cherry piece on each cookie. Bake just until edges are light brown, 20 to 25 minutes. Cool 10 minutes; remove from foil. **About 4 dozen cookies**

PER COOKIE: Calories 30; Protein 0 g; Carbohydrate 5 g; Fat 1 g; Cholesterol 0 mg; Sodium 20 mg

Individual Cranberry-Orange Desserts

Individual Cranberry-Orange Desserts

3 egg whites
1 egg yolk
½ cup skim milk
2 teaspoons grated orange peel
¼ cup orange juice
1 cup sugar
⅓ cup all-purpose flour
¼ teaspoon salt
¾ cup cranberry halves

Heat oven to 350°. Beat egg whites in large bowl on high speed until stiff peaks form. Beat egg yolk slightly in medium bowl on medium speed. Beat in milk, orange peel and orange juice. Beat in sugar, flour and salt until smooth. Stir in cranberry halves.

Fold egg yolk mixture into egg whites. Divide among 4 ungreased 10-ounce ramekins or custard cups. Place ramekins in rectangular pan, 13 × 9 × 2 inches, on oven rack. Pour very hot water (1 inch deep) into pan. Bake about 30 minutes or until golden brown. Serve warm or cold. Sprinkle lightly with powdered sugar if desired. **4 servings**

PER SERVING: Calories 275; Protein 5 g; Carbohydrate 62 g; Fat 2 g; Cholesterol 55 mg; Sodium 200 mg

Capped Fig Cookies

Fig Filling (below)
1 cup packed brown sugar
⅓ cup margarine, softened
¼ cup buttermilk
2 egg whites
1¾ cups all-purpose flour
1 teaspoon vanilla
½ teaspoon baking soda
½ teaspoon salt
⅛ teaspoon ground cinnamon

Heat oven to 400°. Prepare Fig Filling. Mix brown sugar, margarine, buttermilk and egg whites in large bowl. Stir in remaining ingredients. Drop dough by teaspoonfuls about 2 inches apart onto ungreased cookie sheet. Top each with ½ teaspoon filling. Top filling with ½ teaspoon dough. Bake 8 to 10 minutes or until almost no identation remains when touched (do not touch filling). Immediately remove from cookie sheet; cool. Store tightly covered.
About 3 dozen cookies

Fig Filling

1 cup finely chopped dried figs (about 8)
⅓ cup sugar
¼ cup water
1 tablespoon lemon juice
3 tablespoons chopped walnuts

Heat figs, sugar, water and lemon juice in 1-quart saucepan over medium heat, stirring constantly, until mixture thickens and boils. Stir in walnuts; cool.

PER COOKIE: Calories 80; Protein 1 g; Carbohydrate 15 g; Fat 2 g; Cholesterol 0 mg; Sodium 75 mg

Cherry Clafouti

Clafouti is a casual French country dessert that's an easy ending to a family meal.

3 eggs
1 cup milk
½ cup all-purpose flour
¼ cup granulated sugar
1 teaspoon vanilla
2 cups pitted dark sweet cherries
Powdered sugar

Heat oven to 350°. Grease square baking dish, 8 × 8 × 2 inches. Beat eggs, milk, flour, granulated sugar and the vanilla with hand beater until smooth. Spread cherries in dish. Pour batter over cherries. Bake 45 to 50 minutes or until puffed and golden brown. Sprinkle with powdered sugar. Serve warm.   **6 servings**

PER SERVING: Calories 170; Protein 6 g; Carbohydrate 29 g; Fat 4 g; Cholesterol 110 mg; Sodium 50 mg

Grape Gumdrops

You can cut gumdrops into different shapes, just as you would cookies. Use small cookie or canapé cutters dipped in sugar, or cut them freehand.

Vegetable oil
1 cup sugar
1 cup light corn syrup
¾ cup grape juice
1 package (1¾ ounces) powdered fruit
  pectin
½ teaspoon baking soda
2 drops blue food color, if desired
Sugar

Line loaf pan, 9 × 5 × 3 inches, with aluminum foil. Brush with oil. Heat 1 cup sugar and the corn syrup to boiling in 1½-quart saucepan over medium-high heat, stirring constantly, until sugar is dissolved. Cook, without stirring, to 280° on candy thermometer or until small amount of mixture dropped into very cold water separates into hard but not brittle threads.

While cooking sugar mixture, heat grape juice, pectin and baking soda to boiling (mixture will be foamy) in 2-quart saucepan over high heat, stirring constantly; reduce heat.

Slowly pour hot sugar mixture in a thin stream into grape juice mixture, stirring constantly (this should take 1 to 2 minutes); remove from heat. Stir in food color. Let stand 2 minutes. Skim off foam.

Pour mixture into pan. Let stand uncovered at room temperature 24 hours. Lift foil from pan and remove foil from sides. Cut into ¾-inch squares with knife dipped into sugar. Roll squares in sugar. Let stand uncovered at room temperature 1 hour. Store gumdrops in airtight container.   **72 gumdrops**

ORANGE GUMDROPS: Substitute orange juice for the grape juice and red food color for the blue food color.

APPLE-CHERRY GUMDROPS; Substitute apple-cherry drink for the grape juice and red food color for the blue food color.

PER GUMDROP: Calories 28; Protein 0 g; Carbohydrate 7 g; Fat 0 g; Cholesterol 0 mg; Sodium 10 mg

Taffy

You don't have to go to the seaside for great saltwater taffy. Salt water isn't even a necessary ingredient; fresh water works wonderfully (no matter what they tell you down on the boardwalk). Use different extracts to create your favorite flavors.

1 cup sugar
1 tablespoon cornstarch
¾ cup light corn syrup
⅔ cup water
2 tablespoons margarine or butter
1 teaspoon salt
2 teaspoons vanilla
¼ teaspoon food color, if desired

Butter square pan, 8 × 8 × 2 inches. Mix sugar and cornstarch in 2-quart saucepan. Stir in corn syrup, water, margarine and salt. Heat to boiling over medium heat, stirring constantly. Cook, without stirring, to 265° on candy thermometer or until small amount of mixture dropped into very cold water forms a hard ball that holds its shape but is pliable; remove from heat. Stir in vanilla and food color. Pour into pan.

When just cool enough to handle, pull taffy with lightly buttered hands until satiny, light in color and stiff. Pull into long strips ½ inch wide. Cut strips into 1½-inch pieces with scissors. (For ease in cutting, wipe scissors with vegetable oil.) Wrap pieces individually in plastic wrap or waxed paper (candy must be wrapped to hold its shape). **About 4 dozen candies**

ALMOND TAFFY: Stir in 2 teaspoons almond extract with the vanilla.

PEPPERMINT TAFFY: Substitute 1 tablespoon peppermint extract for the vanilla. Stir in ¼ teaspoon red food color, if desired, with the peppermint extract.

PER CANDY: Calories 15; Protein 0 g; Carbohydrate 4 g; Fat 0 g; Cholesterol 0 mg; Sodium 45 mg

Mint Wafers

Many people find mints refreshing at the end of a meal. Their mixture of sweetness and coolness can be enjoyed any time.

3½ to 4 cups powdered sugar
⅔ cup sweetened condensed milk
Few drops food color, if desired
½ teaspoon peppermint, spearmint or wintergreen extract

Cover cookie sheet with waxed paper. Mix 3½ cups powdered sugar, the milk and food color. Knead in extract and enough additional powdered sugar to make a smooth, creamy mixture. Shape into 1-inch balls. Place about 1 inch apart on cookie sheet. Flatten each ball with fork to about ¼-inch thickness. Let stand uncovered at room temperature about 1 hour or until firm.

Turn candies over and let stand about 1 hour or until tops are firm. Store mints in airtight container. **About 8 dozen wafers**

CUTOUT MINTS: Divide mixture in half. Shape one half into flattened round on cloth-covered board generously sprinkled with granulated sugar. Roll in sugar to coat. Roll mixture ¼ inch thick. Cut with 1-inch cutters. Place mints on waxed paper. Repeat with remaining mixture. Continue as directed.

PER WAFER: Calories 25 g; Protein 0 g; Carbohydrate 6 g; Fat 0 g; Cholesterol 0 mg; Sodium 5 mg

METRIC CONVERSION GUIDE

U.S. UNITS	CANADIAN METRIC	AUSTRALIAN METRIC
Volume		
1/4 teaspoon	1 mL	1 ml
1/2 teaspoon	2 mL	2 ml
1 teaspoon	5 mL	5 ml
1 tablespoon	15 mL	20 ml
1/4 cup	50 mL	60 ml
1/3 cup	75 mL	80 ml
1/2 cup	125 mL	125 ml
2/3 cup	150 mL	170 ml
3/4 cup	175 mL	190 ml
1 cup	250 mL	250 ml
1 quart	1 liter	1 liter
1 1/2 quarts	1.5 liter	1.5 liter
2 quarts	2 liters	2 liters
2 1/2 quarts	2.5 liters	2.5 liters
3 quarts	3 liters	3 liters
4 quarts	4 liters	4 liters
Weight		
1 ounce	30 grams	30 grams
2 ounces	55 grams	60 grams
3 ounces	85 grams	90 grams
4 ounces (1/4 pound)	115 grams	125 grams
8 ounces (1/2 pound)	225 grams	225 grams
16 ounces (1 pound)	455 grams	500 grams
1 pound	455 grams	1/2 kilogram

Measurements		Temperatures	
Inches	Centimeters	Fahrenheit	Celsius
1	2.5	32°	0°
2	5.0	212°	100°
3	7.5	250°	120°
4	10.0	275°	140°
5	12.5	300°	150°
6	15.0	325°	160°
7	17.5	350°	180°
8	20.5	375°	190°
9	23.0	400°	200°
10	25.5	425°	220°
11	28.0	450°	230°
12	30.5	475°	240°
13	33.0	500°	260°
14	35.5		
15	38.0		

NOTE
The recipes in this cookbook have not been developed or tested using metric measures. When converting recipes to metric, some variations in quality may be noted.

Index

(Page numbers in *italics* indicate photographs.)